HerStory

Life-Changing Lessons

from Women of the Bible

God Bless!

Jacob M. Rodriguez

HerStory
© 2015 by Jacob M. Rodriguez

Published by CityLight Publications
Cover design by Vanessa Cardenas

ISBN-13: 978-1512184037
ISBN-10: 1512184039

Emphasis within Scripture is the author's own. Please note that the author's writing style is to capitalize certain pronouns in Scripture and text that refer to God, and may differ from other religious publishers' styles. The author chose to acknowledge Him, even to the point of violating grammatical rules.

Other Books by Jacob M. Rodriguez:

The Woman's Touch

Someone Like Me

The Lord's Lady

Hidden Kings

Crave

Shift

Lying Lions

Dedication

To my beautiful wife, Cherie. She has shown me that besides every good man is a *better* woman.

Contents

Prologue

Have you ever wished you could talk with one of the characters of the bible? I know I do. Aside from the Lord Jesus Christ, I would love to interview some Old Testament characters like Moses, Abraham, David, or even some of the lesser known. As a woman, I'm sure there are some women you would love to meet too. Well, this is your opportunity. Although their lives are ancient history, their stories still speak today. You may be surprised how much in common you have with them.

In this book, I've chosen seven women to retell their stories, and help you discover God's unbreakable strength. Your first question might be, "Why did you chose these seven women?" To be perfectly honest, as I prepared for this book, these women seemed to leap out of the pages of the bible.

Are they the greatest, and most revered women in scripture? You can confidently argue either way. But I didn't select women who necessarily fit the mold. In fact, you'll notice a common thread in each of their lives. None of them were perfect. Some made huge mistakes, some wasted precious time and others thrived under pressure.

My purpose is to free these biblical women—allowing them to be a canvas for a broader viewpoint of reality. We tend to tidy them up, airbrush their flaws and gloss over their unpredictable behavior. But these women weren't shaped with a cookie-cutter. Nor did they ever volunteer to be the subject of scrutiny. They are authentic, real and true testimonies of God's grace.

I invite you to get comfortable, find a quiet place, and discover seven imperfect women who discovered God's perfect strength.

Chapter 1

Rivalries of Love

Imagine if your husband married you—thinking you were your sister. Then, in a twist of events, you end up married to the same man. Sound like a complete nightmare? For one young lady it was reality. The woman I'm referring to is none other than Leah.

Leah's story is brief, yet compelling. Cast as more of a supporting role, Leah involuntarily becomes the focal point of the entire story. She is introduced at the heart of Jacob's quest for Rachel. Negotiations between Laban (Leah and Rachel's father) and Jacob had already begun. Jacob was head-over-heels for Rachel. You could almost say it was "love at first sight".

To really understand Leah's life, it's good to know a little bit of Jacob's background. Known mostly for his illusive lifestyle, Jacob had found himself on the run from his brother

Esau. After following his mother's advice, he bartered for his brother's birthright, deceived his father, and took a blessing that wasn't his. Then after receiving his father's blessing, he was sent to the region of Padam Aram. It was when he arrived there that he met Rachel.

Jacob and Rachel fell in love. There was no doubt in Jacob's mind that he wanted to marry her. So he agreed to work seven years for her. Most of us would think that's way too long, but for Jacob it was a labor of love.

After this small backdrop, we can continue with Leah's story.

The Other Sister

Genesis 29:16-17 says, *"Now Laban had two daughters: the name of the elder was Leah, and the name of the younger was Rachel. Leah's eyes were delicate, but Rachel was beautiful of form and appearance."* The contrast between Leah and Rachel, and, Esau and Jacob is fascinating.

In both families you have an older sibling who isn't favored like the younger. In both families, the younger steals the elders' blessing. What Jacob was to Esau, Rachel was to Leah. The similarities are interesting and probably not a coincidence. God always has a way of harmonizing his message. Rachel was daddy's little princess. And Leah was the proverbial ugly duckling.

As a girl, Leah knew that her dad played favorites. Even though she was older, she grew up in her younger sister's shadow. Rachel was beautiful, charming and had a smile that could light up a dark room. The Bible describes Rachel as being *"beautiful in form and appearance."* Basically, Rachel was the total package. She was so lovely that Jacob's jaw might have dislocated and dropped to the floor when he saw her.

When Leah is described, the Bible says her *"eyes were delicate"*—a nice way of saying she wasn't very pretty. Leah didn't have the lovely features of her younger sister. However, it wasn't just her physical appearance, but also her heart, her self-image. Leah's "weak" eyes were the windows into her soul. Her eyes were an outward reflection of how she felt about herself.

Leah was insecure about her femininity. A woman's emotions can take a heavy toll on her countenance. When a woman is depressed or insecure, her appearance reflects it. You can only pretend so long until you start resembling your problem. Leah's condition made her undesirable. When Jacob stood there looking at the two sisters, poor Leah looked tired and unhappy.

Leah didn't just feel ugly, she felt like a second-rate woman.

Dear reader, if the enemy can accomplish anything in your life, it's to get you to feel like less of a woman, less of who God created you to be. Inferiority can be troubling setback in a woman's life. A poor self-image can put your potential on a short leash. That's why Satan works overtime to diminish your dignity. That's also why he attacks adolescent girls with sexual abuse and abandonment—so by the time they're grown women, they feel worthless.

The more inferior you feel, the less capable you are of living the life God created you for. When you have an inferiority complex, compliments don't mean very much. Your husband could say, "Honey, you look beautiful", yet when you look in the mirror, you think to yourself, "I hate my body". No matter what he or your children say, you're still not happy who you see in the mirror. Years into the marriage, your husband feels like nothing he ever does or says is good enough.

But in reality, you don't think you're good enough.

Leah didn't start fighting Rachel when they married the same man. The fight began when daddy would swoop up little Rachel in his arms and smother her with kisses. Leah knew something was different and the lack of her father's affection created a huge hole in her heart.

Every woman wants to feel loved, admired, and accepted. She wants to feel like a princess. Leah was no different. She wanted acceptance, but never received it. She wanted a hug, but hardly got one. However, Rachel wasn't the problem, dad was.

If Laban, Leah's father, had poured equal time and affection on both daughters, Leah wouldn't have felt so timid and cheated. Leah's family was unbalanced. But like I mentioned, Rachel was not to blame. She too was an innocent child. It was Laban who created this mess. Of course, Leah didn't see things from this perspective. All she saw was Rachel's beauty and the attention she got. Unbeknownst to her, Leah was really not angry with Rachel, but with her dad. Oftentimes we channel our frustration to the most visible target. In this case, Rachel became just that.

The Daddy Disease

I often see what I would label, "the daddy disease". This describes what happens when a child, in this case—a girl, grows up without a loving father. Dad might have been home, but perhaps he was preoccupied or wasn't intentional about his relationship with you. Maybe he hoped for a boy and never fully embraced you. Maybe he just didn't know how to show affection and struggled to bond with you. The point is that many women grow up without a father. Leah had a similar situation.

I certainly don't want to bash Laban. To his credit, he was present and did provide a godly environment for his family. Otherwise, Isaac would have never recommended that Jacob marry Rachel. Laban wasn't evil, but perhaps misguided and unfair. So he shouldn't be harassed, but understood. As a side note, I believe that pop-culture and even voices in the Christian community have spent too much time "father bashing", and not enough time understanding their fathers. While some criticism is warranted, certain fathers shouldn't be demonized for being imperfect men.

Leah and Rachel were rivals because Laban didn't affirm them equally. I would like to ask you a straightforward question. What was your relationship like with your father? Even if it's difficult, I want you to think about your father.

Who is or, who was he?

I know these questions may fuel different emotions. If your relationship with him is good, you probably have some fond memories. You should feel blessed if your relationship with him was healthy. But if your relationship with him was strained or tense, then you might feel a bit saddened. Maybe your relationship with your dad has improved over time.

The reason I asked you to think about him was because I want you to understand something, even if it's difficult to swallow. If your father caused you pain and made life difficult for you, this pill will be even harder to swallow.

Your father is not the enemy, but Satan is.

People may have told you that he's to blame everything. Your father may have been imperfect, cruel, or just unavailable, but Satan is still the sole conspirator. If you're going to upset with anyone, let it be the enemy. Don't spend another day tearing down a faulty parent. Instead, tear down the kingdom of evil that waged war against your spirit.

Your father was human, capable of being manipulated and hurt. Remember, this doesn't excuse him, but it helps to explain him. The goal is not to defend any guilty party, but to understand how you got here today, and what steps you take tomorrow. Your father is fully responsible for his actions—good or bad. Frankly, just like you are. But resenting him won't do much to improve your life, nor will it nourish your faith in God.

Women who are hurt with their fathers haven't found much satisfaction with resentment. People may have influenced you to target your father and accuse him. But your father is not your enemy, neither is your mother; Satan is. If anyone is to blame, it's him. He was the one who launched the spiritual assault against your life. The Bible says that Satan roams around like a lion, seeking someone to devour.

However you still must be armed with the knowledge and understanding about what exactly your father handed down to you. Unless you face the issues you have inherited, you won't be able to move beyond them—especially women whose father had a negative impact on their lives.

Even though Leah's father wasn't the real enemy, he is still responsible for his own actions. He is far from an innocent bystander.

Laban gave his daughters more than his genes; he passed down a heritage of family dysfunctions. Because of this, both Leah and Rachel struggled to find their place in life. Both got tangled in relational knots and fought for love. Both spent years trying to keep their heads above the waterline of feminine significance and value. Both were afraid of becoming insignificant—all because of how dad treated them.

Can you relate with Leah? Even if your upbringing was healthy and positive, can you empathize with her?

Laban gave a personal assistant named Zilpah to Leah. Zilpah's name means "frail or weary". Even daddy's favorite Rachel got Bilhah as her personal assistant. Bilhah's name means "troubled or timid". Basically, Leah and Rachel inherited weariness, trouble and timidity from their father. Because her dad was weary, Leah became weary. Because her dad was troubled, Leah was troubled. Because her dad was timid and fearful, guess what Leah became?

Laban failed his daughters. And honestly, their mother doesn't get any gold medals here either. Where was she? How come we don't see any motherly defense? What was she scared of? Where does mom fit into this picture? Leah's mother chose to play along and pretend everything was fine.

She probably wanted to keep the peace, even though she saw the dysfunction. Why didn't she demand something better for her daughters?

Anytime you see a problem and do nothing, you become part of the problem. A real mother puts her children first. She steps between her children and danger. She risks her own livelihood to protect her children against any foul play. Laban's wife doesn't get a free pass. After all, this was a family.

Maybe your mom didn't step in for you. Maybe she kept the peace, at the expense of your emotions. She too isn't perfect, nor is she blameless.

Leah was living with the same issues her dad lived with. Sadly, even when he tried to help his daughters, he ended up causing more problems for them. Maybe that describes your relationship with your father to some degree. Even when he tried to help and patch things up, the situation only got worse. His efforts to build a bridge only burned more bridges.

What's the toughest part about all of this?

Perhaps you see a little bit of your dad or mom in you. Maybe you see it in the way you handle relationships, manage conflict, or deal with stress. It could just be your overall attitude about life.

Let me take this opportunity to tell you that no matter what negative characteristic you were given, no matter what curse or issue you inherited, God's will is for you to live free of that. God does not want you to live with the same pattern. Through the love of God, you can overcome any generational issue in your life.

As you'll see in the next chapter, Leah's problems were far from over. It would take quite a few lessons before she discovered God's unbreakable love.

Chapter 2

Here Comes the *Bribe*

Leah's issues at home followed her into marriage. No surprise there. The unresolved, unhealed areas of your past will cling to you until they are completely dealt with.

The deal was done. Jacob had completed his seven years and was ready to make Rachel his bride. His work had finally paid off. However there was only one major problem; the bride he thought he was getting wasn't Rachel, but Leah. Jacob, a trickster himself, was tricked!

This was the start of a painful journey for Leah. When we read this story, we tend to assume that Leah wanted to marry Jacob. We tend to believe that she instantly loved him, and wanted to be his wife. However, Jacob wasn't the only one who got a raw deal.

If anyone got cheated, it was Leah. Nothing suggests that Leah was interested in Jacob; the Bible never mentions that

Leah wanted to be his wife. Rather it seems she just wanted to be someone's wife. Sure, her and Rachel were at odds, but that doesn't mean that she wanted her fiancé.

She wanted to be loved.

Leah was bribed just like Jacob. She was used just like he was. Just because Jacob woke up startled by her, doesn't mean she was comfortable with this bizarre relationship. Let's get this straight. Neither one of them loved each other.

Leah wanted love, but that doesn't mean she was in love with Jacob. Imagine Leah's shock when Laban pitched his plan for her to marry, instead of her sister. Leah felt cheated because in her heart she knew this wasn't her wedding. This wasn't her storybook wish or girlhood dream. She hadn't prepared for this scenario.

I'm sure she thought Jacob was a great man, but not her man.

Imagine how she felt, as her wedding ceremonies were about to begin. She didn't know what to expect. She was scared and worried. On a day that should have been filled with joy, was filled with discomfort. The man who is becoming her husband doesn't even know it yet. How awkward she must have felt!

The wedding continued, and the whole time Leah felt guilty—not only for deceiving Jacob, but for hurting Rachel. Her sister Rachel had to sit back and watch her sister marry the love of her life. Pardon the cliché, but Leah was stuck between a rock and a hard place.

"Just" Married

Then Jacob did so and fulfilled her week. So he gave him his daughter Rachel as wife also. And Laban gave his maid Bilhah to his daughter Rachel as a maid. Then Jacob also went in to Rachel, and he also loved Rachel more than Leah. And he served with Laban still another seven years (Genesis 29:28-30).

Many newlywed couples drive away from their wedding ceremony with the words "just married" written on their car or limousine. When you see a car drive by with those big letters on the back window, you imagine a joyful and giddy couple excited about their new journey together. You imagine a couple deeply in love.

However, for Leah, she wasn't "just married"...but rather "just" married. In other words, she was only—merely married, not lovingly joined with her groom.

The wedding was over. The feast and festivities were finished. The shocking night when Jacob discovered her in his bed was now over. Whether or not Jacob and Leah liked their situation, it was now their life. Even though neither of them asked for this life, they had to make the best of it.

Leah was still in shambles. Even after marriage, unusual as it was, she still faced the same giants she had before saying "I do".

Marriage had not healed the wounds of feeling unloved and unwanted. I wonder how many women find themselves in similar situations? They expected that after the white dress and honeymoon, their emotional wrinkles would simply be ironed out. They hoped that once the picket fence was up and the kitchen smelled like apple pie everything would take care of itself—that somehow the years of unsettled issues would melt with the scented candles in the living room.

God's love must be allowed into your live like never before. You must give him access to the hidden areas of your heart. Like Leah, time and experiences won't change the issues that loom over your life. The powerful love of God is the only remedy that can heal a broken heart.

Secretly, Leah still craved to be accepted and cherished. She hungered for true love. She longed to be treasured and admired. After years of not getting enough from her dad, now she couldn't get much from her husband either. All she did was marry someone like her father. Same old issue, only now it's her husband, not her father, who loves someone more than her. What a terrible feeling it must be to know that your husband is with you, just out of obligation—to your vows, your children or to maintain the "happy family" image. Every woman wants to be loved and cherished by her husband, not a ball-in-chain to some other place he'd rather be.

God Sees You

Genesis 29:31 says, *"When the LORD saw that Leah was unloved, He opened her womb; but Rachel was barren."* God saw that Leah was unloved. He took special notice of her heart and how she had been treated over the years. It's interesting how God sees what man cannot. He's able to peer into the heart and soul, and search the depths of who we are and what we're capable of.

Dear woman, God is looking deep into the chambers of your heart. He sees where you are and what's been missing from your life. The Lord sees even your darkest secrets and hurts.

I cannot stress enough, how important it is, that you realize that God sees you—the real you, the part of you that you've worked tirelessly to cover up. He sees what lies beneath—the area of your heart or past that still keeps you up at night and drains all of your strength. He sees the undertow of emotions, heartaches and frustrations that whirl around in your mind.

Even while others around you are entirely oblivious to your pain and struggles, totally in the dark about what you've been thinking and talking to yourself about, God's eyes have probed that exact area. He sees the tender spots in your heart. He knows where it came from, who caused it, and how you've tried to cope.

As in Leah's case, your parents may not even be aware of what's happening in your life. They may have no idea that you suffered.

No matter where you are today, God sees you. He sees beyond your façade and appearance. He sees that you're still offended, still bothered, still bitter, still broken, still waiting, still crying, still hoping for things to be different. God sees what you cannot explain, cannot express or reveal. He reads the heart and understands your invisible, intangible feelings.

Oftentimes the greatest gift is not just being able to see God, but knowing that He sees you. God sees you for you who are. Not only does God see the hidden struggles and heartaches, but He also sees your hidden potential and dormant gifts. God is an expert in looking at the heart. He doesn't call people based on their outward appearance, but by what he sees on the inside. Nobody knows your potential like God does. He sees what others take years to recognize. Your unseen gifts, abilities, and promises are not hidden from God's eyes. After all, he put those qualities in you when he formed you.

It is so crucial that you understand that God sees you clearly. Leah's heartaches multiplied because she spent far too much time worrying about how others saw her. Like many women, she based most of her self-worth on how others viewed her. She depended too much on other people's opinions about her life—her appearance, her abilities.

It's amazing how much time women waste worrying about what other people think of them. Some women feel like failures if everybody doesn't love, accept or approve them.

Unlike men, women are wired to be relational. And your heart hurts when you feel rejected. Women can handle incredible amounts of pain, such as childbirth. But one thing that has proven to strike women harder than most other pains is rejection. Women often worry too much about how others see them. Like Leah, when your life is about making sure that others love you, you are giving them the power to determine your worth.

Leah's every breath seemed to hinge on how she was seen and accepted by others. However God's message came to her loud and clear. So much so that He healed her barren womb and gave her a son. The bible says, "So Leah became pregnant and gave birth to a son. She named him Reuben, for she said, *"The Lord has noticed my misery..."* (Genesis 29:32, NLT)

The name Reuben means, "See a son". Today, you must recognize that God sees you, which means He's with you. He understands you. God Himself has taken notice of you.

As a born again believer, you have been accepted and affirmed by Jesus Christ! When He sees you, He sees:

- His child (John 1:12)
- His friend (John 15:15)
- His craftsmanship (Eph. 2:10)

The only opinion that matters is the Lord's. How He sees you, is the way you should see yourself. Stop empowering other people to dictate your self-worth. You are who God says you are. Start seeing yourself as God sees you. Start treating yourself as God treats you. Let His precious word be the mirror of your life, the true reflection of your value. Never allow people to hijack your self-image and significance.

Remember who you are in God's eyes.

Leah's healing doesn't stop here. Not only does God see her, but He also hears her.

Chapter 3

Letting God Complete You

She soon became pregnant again and gave birth to another son. She named him Simeon, for she said, "The LORD heard that I was unloved and has given me another son." (Genesis 29:33, NLT)

Few things mean more to a woman than being heard. As a husband, I can recall times when my wife tried to communicate something important to me that I didn't understand. Sure, I was listening to her talk, but I couldn't hear her voice, the meaning behind what she was saying. I quickly learned that nothing is more frustrating to a woman than when she isn't being heard!

As a man, I struggle at times understanding my wife's concerns. Men and women not only think differently, but we communicate and process information differently. It's a dynamic married couples face on a daily basis, especially new couples. Most women can send a complete message without ever opening her mouth. Your body language is seamlessly interwoven with your mood. I can tell when something is bothering my wife, without her saying one word. Just by her demeanor or gestures, I can guess what is on her mind.

Men are limited in our ability to fully understand and grasp your voice. However God is much different. He hears on a frequency that often goes unheard. Leah experienced this first-hand. Nobody around her could tune into her heart's cry for love and worth. Not her father. Not her sister. Not even her husband.

Leah named her second son "Simeon", which means "God heard". This was God saying, "My daughter, I hear you". Leah was trying to be heard. She was talking, but nobody was listening. Her heart was calling out for love and acceptance, but nobody could decode her message. Even if others had heard, they didn't do enough to show interest or concern.

When you sense that no one is listening, you begin to feel isolated, alone on an island. But perhaps it's more like being trapped in a soundproof room with windows. You raise your voice to the highest pitch, hoping to get the attention of someone walking by. The louder you yell for help, the more it seems you can't be heard. People walk by, living their lives without ever hearing your voice.

Sadly, women live this way, perhaps even you. They live in a soundproof box, unable to be heard, many times in their own homes. Leah was a wife and mother—struggling to be heard everyday. Helping her husband, raising children and doing all she's supposed to do, and yet she still feels like no one hears her. Maybe her case was extreme, because she had to share her husband with her sister. But there are still some relevant parallels we can draw from.

Leah was lost in her own house, silent amidst the hustle and bustle of daily life. I wonder, can you relate?

If your husband had a prior relationship and children, maybe you feel like Leah, who constantly had to contend with another female's demands. Maybe you feel that your voice gets forgotten in the tug-of-war between your home and another.

Likewise, you could be on the opposite end, where your ex-husband started another family, and now your concerns have fallen on deaf ears. As you try to hang on to whatever ties still exist (for the children's sake), you find yourself feeling unheard and alone. Your greatest fear could simply be that your voice no longer matters.

Only you know what your soundproof room looks like on a daily basis. Perhaps you're not sharing your husband with another woman or family, but other things can steal his focus. If you have a husband or father who listens to you, consider yourself blessed. Thank God for him.

Every woman's situation is different.

For you, it could be that your husband is hearing you, but your children or family don't listen. Maybe your son or daughter has put you on mute. Every opinion you share is misinterpreted and has you wondering why you can't get through to your kids. No matter how much you voice your thoughts and try to protect your kids, they seem to have earplugs on and only listen to their peers. It's frustrating when you offer motherly advice and your daughter just thinks you're trying to control her.

You're beginning to wonder…"Does anybody hear me?"

The answer to that question is "yes!" God hears you, understands you, and desperately wants to help you. Leah discovered what you should discover today.

God has heard you loud and clear.

He's listening even now. He knows the depths of your heart. He hears the unspoken words and reads your language clearly. Every prayer you pray, and thought you think, God hears it. You are being heard! And most importantly, the One who hears everything in your heart is the one with the power to change your circumstances.

God understands the language of tears. He detects the vibrations in your soul, the longings in your heart. God not only sees you, but He hears you. Even when you thought that no one was listening and your voice fell on deaf ears, God listened. You have God's full attention. He is tuned into your life and records all of your frustrations. The Psalmist David said, *"You keep track of all my sorrows. You have collected all my tears in your bottle. You have recorded each one in your book"* (Psalm 56:8, NLT). This tells you that you are not alone. You are His daughter, and your voice matters.

Leah spent years believing that she was unnoticed and unloved. But God reversed all of that. Remember the scripture you read earlier, *"When the LORD saw that Leah was unloved, He opened her womb..."* (Genesis 29:31). Before I move on to the next phase, I want you to catch something significant. Leah had open wounds, areas of her heart with love-shaped holes and missing pieces. However, what used to be an open wound...was now an open womb. God used the very thing that weakened her, to bless her.

Oftentimes God uses the wounded or broken area of your life to show you that He loves you. He works through our hurts and difficulties to display his perfect strength—a message I hope you receive throughout this entire book. 2 Corinthians 12:9 mentions that *"His strength is made perfect in our weaknesses"*. I believe that as you're reading this book, God is preparing to manifest his power through your life. Don't look to your strengths or abilities. The answer is not in how good or great you are in one particular area of your life. Your open wound will become your open womb, the gateway of God's goodness and mercy.

God has a way of opening up closed doors. He has a way of unlocking the barrenness of your life and manifesting His glory through you. Get ready to experience an opening, an awakening in your spirit.

Completely His

Leah continued to struggle with herself. Even though she was doing better, she wasn't completely free from her thoughts. She knew that God could see her, and hear her, but wasn't quite over the fact that she was still unloved by others. Flashbacks of the wedding still haunted her heart at times. This would be a good time to remind you that healing in the heart doesn't happen overnight. If you can relate to Leah on any level, be it small or large, understand that healing takes time. Don't expect just one blessing, one prayer, or one sermon to magically erase the issues. God is working with you step-by-step, day-by-day.

Leah couldn't help but feel that something was still missing. So, she had a third son.

Then she became pregnant a third time and gave birth to another son. She named him Levi, for she said, "Surely this time my husband will feel affection for me, since I have given him three sons!" (Genesis 29:34, NLT).

Leah named her third son "Levi", which means "joined". In her mind, this was another opportunity woo her husband. This was a third attempt to connect with a husband who was emotionally detached. All she wanted was for them to be a real couple. However, this was one of God's ways to show Leah her need for a relationship with Him. God could be blessing you, and you still try to measure up to something that isn't going to return the favor. The time has come for you to realize that it's God who wants to be joined to your life.

Don't misinterpret his blessings. He's not blessing you so that you can keep banging your head against same wall. He's not healing you so that you can make the same mistakes and wish for the things that won't work.

God is asking for you to wake up and see that it's Him you need to cling to, love, and cherish. Embrace God's love for you today. He's trying to show you that He loves you. Open your eyes to His care in your life. God knows that you still desire acceptance from others. He knows that you still want certain things to be fixed. He knows your prayers, your desires and your hopes.

However, until you learn to embrace the love of One you cannot see, you won't be able to embrace the love of those you can see.

Leah was persistent. She was relentless. I'll give her that. But she demanded something that even if Jacob were to embrace her, she still wouldn't receive. That's right. Even if Jacob had embraced Leah, it wouldn't have been enough. What Leah needed to see, and what you need to see today, is that only God can complete you! Only the Lord Jesus Christ can complete who you are as a woman. Not your husband. Not your children. Not your friends.

No one else but God can fill the gaps in your life.

The problem some women have is that they've only heard that God loves them, but haven't embraced his love through a personal relationship with Him. Hearing that God loves you is not the same as experiencing His love. As Paul noted (Ref Eph. 3:16-19), you need to experience how wide, how long, how high, and how deep God's love for you is. Then, and only then, you will be made complete with all the fullness of life.

Do you want to live life to the fullest? Do you want to plug the holes that drain your heart?

If so, it's time to embrace God's love. Don't bother trying to woo Him with how good you are. You don't need to impress God, or fight for his attention. Just be the woman God created you to be. Free yourself from worry, and allow the Lord to complete you with His love.

Start living your life as God's beloved woman.

Adjusting your Attitude

Leah finally realized that she couldn't put her life on hold any longer. She decided not to wait around for people to accept her. This change in Leah's heart became evident when she gave birth to her fourth son whom she named "Judah", meaning "praise". Genesis 29:35 (NLT) says, *"Once again Leah became pregnant and gave birth to another son. She named him Judah, for she said, "Now I will praise the Lord!" And then she stopped having children."*

Between Levi and Judah, something happened inside of Leah. A change occurred in her attitude and spirit. This isn't the same Leah—worried about who loves her and who doesn't. We see a different woman here, a woman who decided to embrace God and herself. Maybe you're wondering, "What happened to her?"

Leah's environment didn't change. Jacob was still emotionally unavailable. Rachel was still his number one priority. Laban, her father, was no longer involved. By all accounts, Leah still had reason to be bitter, upset and frustrated. She could have continued to make the home uneasy and difficult to live in.

Leah could have stirred up more trouble, more controversy in the family. Remember that it's the woman who sets the emotional temperature in the home. You are your family's thermostat.

The situation didn't change. Leah changed. She changed her outlook by making some important decisions. First, she embraced God's love. Second, she adjusted her attitude. People like to complain, because it's less painful than change. If you change, it requires effort. It means confronting a side of you that has possibly grown out of control.

Leah could have kept complaining. That's the sinkhole many women get stuck in. There are women who still complain about stuff that happened years ago. In fact, certain women will waste 80% of the good to complaining about the 20% that's bad.

What sense does that make?

You spoil the goodness in life (usually around 80%), complaining and bickering about the bad stuff (usually only 20%). That's exactly where the devil has trapped some women. They can't enjoy the blessings they do have, because they're too disappointed about what they don't have.

They complain their husband's 20% negative attributes, instead of enjoying and appreciating the 80% of his positive attributes. They complain about their jobs, based on the 20%. They complain about their churches, based on the 20%. This is a trap. And I urge you to be on the lookout. Don't let that 20% rob you of the love, peace and goodness of God.

Turn your complaints into praise!

Make a decision to praise God for the breath you're breathing. Thank Him for the real horror that he saved you from! Imagine how awful life would have been without the Lord. Think about where you would be if He hadn't scooped you up in His mighty arms. Complaining is for women who don't truly know God. People who haven't discovered the power of praise and worship tend to complain.

Praise is the sign that your attitude has changed.

Notice I didn't say that it's a sign your situation has changed. Praise is not predicated on your circumstances. It's a decision—an attitude. Leah made an intentional choice to glorify God, and to stop glorifying her problems.

"She stopped having children" because she stopped caring about everyone else's opinions. She stopped trying to impress people. She stopped comparing herself with other women. Now, she simply praised God. She became grateful for giving birth to four healthy boys. It's incredible how we can overlook the healthy areas of our lives by focusing all of our attention on the unhealthy—which is sometimes unchangeable.

Have you neglected your healthy relationships because of one that's unhealthy?

How tragic it would have been if Leah had ignored her strong and healthy boys. Sadly that's what some women do. They overlook the strength and goodness of God. That is precisely how dysfunctions get handed down to the next generation.

I encourage you to learn from Leah. Take an honest look at yourself and decide which areas you can turn complaints into praise. I'm not saying to praise God for your heartaches and struggles. I'm suggesting that you praise God despite your heartaches and struggles. Any time you feel a complaint rising, that's your cue to praise the Lord.

Chapter 4

When Love Broke the Rules

God loves you. In spite of your past, He yearns to feel the touch and the reach of your heart. His love is gracious in times of need, merciful in times of judgment, healing in times of pain, comforting in times of grief. He loves you and wants a personal relationship with you. Although God is King of Kings, His passion for you is informal and real. He wants a genuine relationship with you.

I hope to challenge you to enter a deeper relationship with God—one that is intimate.

Allow me to paint a portrait of what God's love for you is really about. Although God's love almost defies explanation, I know of one woman who realizes the power it holds. If tears were ink, and moments were pages, her life would tell the story of God's unbreakable love.

Her name was Gomer—a woman who was far from perfect, but found perfect strength.

Encased in the Old Testament book of Hosea is an enthralling testimony of God's boundless love. Surrounded by prophecies, national crisis, and God's dealing with Israel is a shocking expression of His ability to love without measure.

Odd Couple

Hosea was a young prophet, a vibrant man of God. He lived a clean life, one that was defined by purity and morality. So I can imagine that God's choice for Hosea's wife must have come as an utter shock.

God didn't select for him a virgin, a princess, or a royal bride. Hosea married a woman with a tainted reputation.

Hosea was a preacher, a man of faith and principles. Certainly if Hosea were to marry, his bride would be as pure as white linen and as gentle as a dove—a sanctified woman for a sanctified man. However, God wrote a much darker love story. On the roughest street, in the filthiest part of town, stood Gomer, Hosea's future wife.

Gomer was a prostitute—a woman paid to perform sexual acts with men. She was a street woman who was caught up in extremely risky behavior. Her life was blotted with failure, marred with misuse, and stained with the ink of sin. With such a low-class status, Gomer wasn't the ideal wife. She was far from it.

Who would desire a woman like this? What kind of prophet would gamble his ministry, his life, to seek someone like Gomer? Who could love this unlovable woman? Who could propose to such a lady? Well, someone did. God compelled Hosea's love towards Gomer, even when she was unlovable. Imagine that, a holy and sanctified man falling in love with a scandalous woman. Yet, he saw beyond her iniquity. He saw the woman behind the blemishes. He found the soul beneath the worn spirit.

Hosea could see the beauty beneath the bruises. When Hosea looked into Gomer's eyes, he saw more than what she used to be, he saw what she would become.

Gomer's life was stained with shame. What could she offer such a holy man? The reality was that she didn't have much to offer. She wasn't qualified to engage in a relationship with a prophet.

When Hosea chose Gomer, he chose her based on his merit, not hers. When he loved her, he stood on his own holiness, not hers. Gomer was hopelessly unholy. However, God doesn't love us based on our merit and righteousness. The Lord didn't submit to a rugged cross and lay His life down because we were holy and blameless. He did it because He loves us, and it's through His righteousness that we have fellowship with Him.

Any argument against Gomer was no longer an issue. Out of the dust of infirmity came the beauty of intimacy. Gomer, who was used to being treated like second-hand clothes, was now the finest fabric in Hosea's life.

I wonder, what made Gomer so irresistible in Hosea's eyes? How did these opposites attract? He wasn't hypnotized or tricked into loving her. There was something about her, something that captured his heart and caused it to melt like warm butter. After all, it was Hosea who pursued Gomer, not the other way around. Much like Christ toward us, Hosea's love for Gomer preceded her love for him. He saw something in her that he decided he couldn't live without. His love for her wasn't fake or driven by pity for her condition. No matter how good of a life you lived, your spiritual condition was just like Gomer's—hopeless. God risked his heavenly reputation and took a chance on love. He hung on the cross for your sins, with no guarantee that you would love him back.

He didn't choose you because you were so good. He chose you because he's so good!

The Risk of Loving Again

Relationships were a sensitive subject for Gomer. The thought of a man sincerely loving a woman was a foreign concept. Gomer's personal experiences formed in her a bias against love. Her occupation required her to block out her emotions. She basically tried to unplug her heart from her behavior. That's simply impossible.

To Gomer, love was a myth, a mystery that no real woman could ever find. Her perception of intimacy was skewed, severely thwarted by her lifestyle. Every sexual encounter left her heart bleeding on the floor. All she had known were the jagged lusts of men who cared nothing about love. She had been touched but not caressed, handled but not held. Gomer wasn't the kind of woman you took home to meet mom. She wasn't the woman with whom a man would fall in love, marry and start a family. The grim reality she lived was anything but healthy. With all of these issues, the concept of true intimacy not only baffled her, but frightened her.

Because of her lifestyle, the idea of receiving an invitation to love seemed ridiculous. After having experienced what a husband and wife experience physically, an authentic relationship was taboo.

What made Hosea or his proposal any different? If you go too long seeing things backward, you start believing that is the way it should be. Your false perception of reality becomes truth to you.

Many women cannot accept love from others because they view of love through the lenses of the past. Love reminds them of a broken heart, divorce, bad timing, disappointment, or even death.

If you're single and a good man shows interest in you, you may push him away—not for anything he has done, but because of what someone did five or ten years ago.

Most women who have been hurt either push away or punish their current relationships. To push is to drive him away, ignore his gestures, or disregard his feelings. To punish is to penalize him for what happened in your previous relationship, to make him pay for what someone else did.

Either way, you lose out on something beautiful in the present. It's likely that when Gomer saw Hosea, she figured he was just like every other man who had ever approached her. Nevertheless, this man was different. Her thoughts would have been similar to the Samaritan woman at the well, who made the mistake of thinking Jesus was just like every other man.

Like Gomer, you too must realize that the One standing before you is different from the rest. Perhaps others were interested only in what they could take from you; Jesus Christ is interested in what He can give you.

Gomer received an invitation, and she accepted. But accepting the invitation was just the beginning. Even though Gomer married Hosea, she still had personal issues to resolve. She was still dealing with much of the rejection she had spent so much of her life trying to handle. Even though she was married to Hosea, she allowed her past to pull her back.

Although she was a wife now, she didn't feel like a wife material. Although she was treated like a princess, she didn't feel like one. No matter what Hosea did for her, her self-perception was still unhealthy. Accepting Hosea was one thing; accepting herself was another. It's impossible to hate yourself and love another. You can give only what's inside of you. Gomer had issues because she tried hard to love Hosea while hating herself at the same time.

Trying to love God while hating yourself will leave your heart bleeding. Truly accepting His love releases you to love yourself and others.

For instance, a wife who loves herself is happier and healthier because she takes care of herself. In turn, this makes her husband happier. You have to be comfortable in your own skin to be able to nurture your relationships, especially your relationship with God.

To be secure in God's love, you must be able to love and accept yourself. One of Gomer's most challenging hurdles was the struggle to rest in Hosea's love. With the echoes of past hurts and failed relationships, she led a lifestyle with her guards up. Accepting the invitation was just the beginning. Gomer had to learn to accept herself.

After suffering years of rejection, her self-worth was low. Gomer squandered her worth. She sold her meaningfulness not just for money, but to avoid being alone.

No More Hiding

Gomer had to overcome a lot in her life. She had to face the skeletons in the closet, perhaps the forces that led down a destructive path. All we can do is assume that something or someone had a negative impact on her. Either way, she's in a different element now. She went from a street woman, to a preacher's wife. There's no doubt that God did a miracle in her life. She was headed nowhere, but God reversed her condition and blessed her with a godly husband.

All seemed blissful until she had a major meltdown. She fell back into the same issues that she hoped to never see again. After hitting rock bottom, her faithful husband redeemed her from the slave block and gave her a second chance.

This time, he was very specific about what changes needed to happen in order for their marriage to work. He said, *"You must live in my house for many days and stop your prostitution. During this time, you will not have sexual relations with anyone, not even with me."* (Hosea 3:3, NLT).

In order for healing and restoration to last in your life, you must make deliberate changes to how you live. This is the step people often overlook. Simply being happy that you are free from your past isn't enough to keep you free. You must make spiritual and practical changes to your life. Neglecting to change will give the enemy opportunities to destroy your hopes. The reason is because he will pick on the same habits and issues that hurt you in the first place.

Paul told the Galatians, *"Stand fast therefore in the liberty by which Christ has made us free, and do not be entangled again with a yoke of bondage."* (Gal. 5:1). Although his counsel deals with Jewish Christians who could easily slip back into the Law of Moses, the principle applies to other areas of life. People have the tendency to slip back into the places where they were rescued.

Why?

Satan knows which buttons to push in your life. He knows which strings to tug on. If you struggled with anger or fear in the past, chances are that Satan will strike the same area again. This is why your mentality must change.

Romans 12:2 says, *"And do not be conformed to this world, but be transformed by the renewing of your mind, that you may prove what is that good and acceptable and perfect will of God."* Gomer struggled so much because even though she was in a good house, she still had some bad habits. Just because she changed her address, got a makeover, and got a new husband, didn't mean that she was free from her past. That's why she couldn't see God's good, acceptable and perfect will.

The same is true for women today.

God needs to change your mindset. Being in church doesn't automatically change your habits, desires and way of thinking.

Even if you grew up in church, went to Sunday school and married a Christian—that doesn't mean you don't have changes to make. Sometimes it's the lifelong Christians who struggle the most because they don't easily recognize the old self. It's harder to come clean about your true habits, issues and mistakes because of religious pressure.

It's difficult convincing Christian women that they need to be transformed; and that salvation isn't conversion. You might be saved, but that doesn't mean you're converted and changed. Gomer was among the clergy. Her new friends had convictions and ministries. Her husband was a well-known prophet. Yet, she had secret issues.

While her husband was praying, ministering and preaching, she was fighting urges to return to her old self. It breaks my heart to know that certain women are sitting in the pews, but afraid to come out and be healed.

God wants to renew your mind and change the kind of woman you are. He wants you to live life without regrets.

Chapter 5

Taking Second Chances

My purpose is not to simply retell Gomer's story, open up some issues, and then leave you wondering, "What next?" Often times we expose problems without learning from them. This chapter is about maximizing second chances. That means learning from your past, so that your future is better and brighter.

Too many women get healed or set free, only to regress. With that said, I would like to suggest four steps that will help you make the most of your second chances.

Step One: Assess your Situation

Properly assessing your situation is crucial to avoiding a repeat. You must ask yourself, "What went wrong? How did I end up here?" Instead of just crediting the devil for ruining something or everything in your life, assess the events, decisions or circumstances that helped to create your problem. Ask yourself, how much of what happened was self-inflicted? Or, am I an innocent bystander?

After an automobile accident, a police officer has to assess the entire situation. He investigates the tire tread marks or scuffs on the roadway, the direction the vehicles traveled, and how fast they moved. Then of course, he needs to see if any laws were broken, and who had the right away. To better understand what happened, he may even interview some eyewitnesses.

It's time to think objectively. This won't be easy. Especially if you feel that you had no control over your situation. Using an automobile accident as a metaphor, here are some tips you can follow.

A. Investigate the tread marks and road signs

Learn the most you can about what lead up to your mistake or misfortune. Ask yourself, "Did anybody warn me? Did I see any red flags before things fell apart? Did I ignore the signs?" Perhaps you were so consumed in the moment that you didn't think much of the signs. Perhaps you thought you could outwit the warnings and change the situation later. Think about your state-of-mind. Were you open-minded, or close-minded? What blinded your vision and better judgment?

It's important for you give an honest look at the tread marks and road signs before you collided with disappointment. Often times, tread marks indicate how fast you went. Is it possible that a relationship moved way too fast; and you didn't have time to get to know each other's habits and temperaments? Maybe you thought onlookers were unfair, judgmental and nosey. But five years and one kid later you aren't so sure you picked the right spouse.

Maybe you jumped into a career too quick—without considering the toll it would take on your family. Whenever someone asked why you worked so late, you took offense and reminded them of who "pays the bills". Maybe your husband gave you clues that he was unhappy, but you thought he was being immature or overreacting. These are examples of tread marks and road signs.

You must investigate your past in order to inform your present. Ask God to help you understand and assess your situation. If you take an honest look at things, God will honor you and trust you enough to bless you again.

B. Identify the laws that were broken

Take a closer look at the guidelines in God's word you might have overlooked or chosen to ignore. The word of God is a guide, a code of principles to live by. It's possible that you disobeyed a direct principle and decided to take your chances. What sins can you easily identify and guard yourself from in the future? Did you lie, cheat, gossip, get jealous or get bitter? Remember, this exercise is not about reliving the past, but assessing it so that you can protect your future. Knowledge is power. Proverbs 24:5 says, *"A wise man has great power, and a man of knowledge increases strength;"*

You cannot conquer what you do not confront. Few things trouble the devil more then when you start confronting the root issues in your life. Without pulling the root, the weed of issues will continue to sprout—no matter how many times you slice the surface. So, instead of having your issues "trimmed" every couple of years, pull that thing out by the root.

C. Interview the witnesses

Maybe you need to talk with an unbiased witness—someone who saw your situation unfold. They can offer you some insight from the outside looking in. Don't be afraid to hear the truth. When you only talk with those involved in your affairs (family, best friends) they tend to side with you and not point out your errors. They don't want to upset you.

An unbiased witness is someone who isn't benefited either way. Talking with an unbiased person helps you think objectively, and not emotionally. When making a life-changing decision, it's always good to talk to a neutral friend or mentor. They level you're thinking and help you see both sides. Additionally, they can tell you the truth, without worrying about hurting your friendship.

They have to be far enough to be unbiased, yet close enough to know you and care about your wellbeing. When they speak, have an open mind.

Assessing your situation is thinking clearly about who you are and how you got where you are today. Sort things out to the best of your ability. This is not about reliving your past, but assessing things from a knowledge standpoint. It's about taking emotional inventory on your life, so you can see what's been lost and gained.

Once you assess your situation, you can move on to the second step.

Step Two: Accept Responsibility

If you only identify what others did, and not yourself, you won't really learn from the experience. You must accept responsibility for your own actions. This isn't to shift all blame on you, or assume that you entirely caused things to fall apart. Rather, this is to be honest about where you played a role, and learn how to avoid that role in the future.

Again, you need ask yourself some tough questions. Such as: How did my behavior, attitude or mindset contribute? What role did I play? We often bypass this step because we're afraid to admit when we're wrong. However, by taking responsibility for your actions, you can address self-destructive patterns in your life. Learn what types of problems you tend to bring upon yourself. Maybe it's time to address your attitude of helplessness, where you pretend there's nothing you can do. Perhaps it's time to quit certain habits or activities that always leave you empty. Figure out why you are attracted to the wrong kinds of friends.

Even if you were mistreated in the past, you still must own your actions today. Because a parent might have mistreated, that doesn't give you a free pass to mistreat your children, or to be unfriendly.

It's so much easier to blame others—to complain about what you didn't get, who didn't support you, who didn't love you and who did you wrong. Perhaps you're married and have your own children now. Maybe you're a grandmother. Either way, it's time to take responsibility for your part, even if it's small.

Let me share a secret with you. The main reason it so hard to accept responsibility is because being a victim has payoffs. As long as you're a victim, you're not obligated to change. But the moment you take responsibility for your actions, you realize that you cannot remain the same.

This is why certain women keep making the same mistakes, over and over again. They don't accept responsibility for their behavior, and thus they don't change themselves for the better. The apostle Paul once wrote, *"Pay careful attention to your own work, for then you will get the satisfaction of a job well done, and you won't need to compare yourself to anyone else. For we are each responsible for our own conduct"* (Galatians 6:4-5, NLT).

I know my advice isn't too warm, but it's what you need in order to live in victory. Now is not the time to be over-emotional. You need concrete, bible-based tactics to deal with the daily threats against your feminine soul. Too many women are just feeling sorry for themselves.

Show the enemy you're not afraid to accept responsibility. Because by doing so, you allow God to heal and restore you.

Step Three: Admit your Weaknesses

Most of us, men and women, hate to admit weakness. It humbles you and reminds you that you're still human. It means owning up to who you are as a person; to think honestly about what you're capable of. As tough as you are, unfortunately you are not superwoman.

If you bang your elbow hard enough, it's going to swell and eventually bruise. If you overload your schedule, and leave little or no time for rest, chances are you will drain your energy. That's the reality of life.

The longtime myth that if you admit weakness, you accept defeat—is simply untrue. Admitting your limitations and weaknesses will actually prepare you for success. How, you ask? The reason is because God uses our weaknesses to reveal His perfect strength. This allows Him to make up the difference in our lives.

Coming to terms with your own humanness is part of realizing the power of your destiny. Take Moses for instance. Moses was the man who God chose to deliver his people out of bondage, and speak on His behalf. He is considered one of the most important figures, not only for his heroic leadership, but for his role in changing the landscape of biblical history.

Yet even Moses faced-off with his own personal flaws and inabilities. Moses had a stuttering problem, and the very thought of standing in front of Pharaoh and declaring Israel's independence, made him extremely nervous.

When God called Jeremiah, he felt totally inadequate because of his young age. Being young and inexperienced, Jeremiah quickly came face-to-face with his own limitations. However in both cases, God confirmed His influence and assured them that they wouldn't be alone.

My point is simply this: admit your weaknesses so that God can position you in His strength. And also, if you don't admit them, they are likely to have greater impact. God wants to help you reach your destination in life, but he needs for you to be honest about yourself. Weaknesses are often blessings in disguise. Here are three hidden blessings:

A. Weakness teaches you to depend on God

Nothing teaches you dependence on God like human weakness and limitation. Too many women spend their time complaining and praying for God to eliminate their weakness. Instead, thank God for them, because through weakness you gain a greater appreciation of God's grace. You realize that it's not you, but God who provides your every need. It's God who sustains you and keeps you from stumbling.

2. Weakness is an opportunity for God's power

God works through our weaknesses. He sees them as opportunities to manifest His power and assure us that His Spirit is at work in our lives. The apostle Paul said, *"And He said to me, "My grace is sufficient for you, for My strength is made perfect in weakness." Therefore most gladly I will rather boast in my infirmities, that the power of Christ may rest upon me"* (2 Corinthians 12:9). The weaker you are, the stronger He is.

3. Weakness prevents pride in the heart

Recognizing your weaknesses can also be the most effective defense against pride. As you know, pride can devastate your potential. It's a disease of the heart that contaminates your character and slowly brings you down.

However, when you admit your weakness, it humbles your spirit and reminds you that you're only human. What makes you a special woman is not that you're perfect (physically or emotionally), but rather that a "perfect" God created you.

Failure to admit weaknesses keeps you discontent—always trying to prove that you are better. It's what causes women to spend thousands of dollars on cosmetic surgery, instead of embracing who she is. It's not only the fact that she can't admit her weaknesses, it's that she can't accept imperfections.

Step Four: Appraise your True Worth

Gomer didn't love herself — she didn't even like herself. Each shameful experience dug for her a deeper hole of self-resentment. It was a risk for Hosea to love her, but in Gomer's eyes; it was a huge risk to accept his love. Because she had her fair share of heartbreaks, she would have wondered whether or not this new man was any different from the rest.

What guarantee did she have that say she wouldn't be hurt again?

Hosea's love was met with rejection. She couldn't handle true love. Something about it frightened her. Hosea's love was so real, so authentic, that she feared she couldn't measure up. It wasn't until Gomer realized her own value that she fully embraced this relationship.

No amount of love will affect your life until you realize your personal value. No measure of affection will comfort a woman until she learns to love herself. If you can't love and accept yourself, what hope does the love of another have— even God? When a woman has not accepted herself, she compensates for it by looking for the acceptance of others. Certain women waste their potential and walk away from God's love, not because God didn't accept them but because they never accepted themselves. They can't get past their own self-image. They can't see themselves as God sees them.

Its time for total deliverance, not just from the offender, but from one's self. Oftentimes, it's your own self-view that cripples your relationships and stunts your spiritual growth. Dear woman, it's time to loose yourself and untangle the limitations you've created.

Forgive yourself.

Free yourself from you.

Your ideas, philosophies and mindsets can keep you from enjoying life. A poor attitude alone can spoil your blessings and reject the support you need.

Stop holding yourself hostage to things that you have no control over, such as your past and irreversible circumstances. Stop punishing yourself for what you did, or who you used to be. Stop thinking that you don't deserve better.

Give yourself a second chance. Allow yourself to be human and imperfect. Give yourself time to work things out and pray about God's purpose for your life. Not everyone is trying to use you. Not everyone has secret motives and is out to take advantage of you. Refuse to let your attitude push another person or blessing away.

Give yourself cushion to heal and love again. Don't judge yourself for small mistakes. Shake things off and keep on going. Free yourself from you!

It's possible that you have become the hardest person to please. Not others, but you, make yourself the hardest woman to satisfy. You can't expect anyone else to accept you, if you can't accept and love yourself. Remove the negative label off your own life. The apostle Paul told the Romans, *"So now there is no condemnation for those who belong to Christ Jesus. And because you belong to him, the power of the life-giving Spirit has freed you from the power of sin that leads to death"* (Romans 8:1-2, NLT).

If you are in Christ, all blame and reproach is removed from your life. The innocent blood of Jesus has washed you clean from the guilt of sin. Therefore, allow yourself to love again, to live again. Maximize your second chances.

Don't doubt yourself another day. The last thing you want to do is second-guess who you are when it matters most. What a tragedy it would be to doubt yourself at one of life's important crossroads. It's that last-second doubt and hesitation that causes collisions with oncoming challenges. Too many times we get right to the edge of destiny, then pull back or stall. Don't allow your past to bully your potential. Rest in God's unconditional love.

Chapter 6

Tearful Goodbyes

You have something that God wants. The catch is—it's within you. Perhaps nobody knows this better than the woman I'm about to reveal. Without her sacrifice, the history books would have to be rewritten. I'm referring to none other than Jochebed, the esteemed mother of Moses.

At first glance, you might be thinking, "Who is that?" If so, don't be embarrassed. Other than the traditional Sunday school lesson, her name isn't mentioned too often. In fact, it's possible that you're hearing her name for the first time. I admit—I nearly forgot about her. However, once I reread her story, I gained a newfound appreciation for the kind of woman she was.

Not only that, but I also gained a wealth of insight we can capture from her example—especially mothers. You'll soon know why.

There's no question that Moses was one of the greatest biblical heroes. Other than Jesus Christ, it's likely that more books and movies have been created about Moses than any other biblical figure. He was chosen to be the deliverer of Israel. But, greatness isn't coincidental. Moses had a mother who pushed him in the direction.

Long before Moses ever marched up to Pharaoh's throne and demanded freedom for Israel, there was Jochebed, who pushed his little basket towards to the Egyptian palace. Years before Moses ever stretched out his hand over the Red Sea and lead God's people to the other side, his mother stretched her faith in God's ultimate plan.

Before Moses became God's servant, he was Jochebed's son. Allow me to paint a picture of a woman who realized her unflinching courage.

No *Good* in Goodbye

Pharaoh's daughter said to her, "Take this baby and nurse him for me, and I will pay you." So the woman took the baby and nursed him. When the child grew older, she took him to Pharaoh's daughter and he became her son. She named him Moses, saying, "I drew him out of the water" (Exodus 2:9-10, NIV).

Jochebed's heart pounded as she carefully nestled her baby in the basket. Swooping the basket up in her arms, she crouched and staggered slowly towards the riverbank.

"Miriam," she whispered.

"Yes mommy."

"Go stand over there behind the brush and be on the look out."

"Okay."

Knee-deep in the marsh of the Nile—her arms wobbled with worry, and her breath rattled in and out. All the courage she felt the night before seemed to abandon her. Second thoughts began to blow through her mind.

"What if I just seclude him?"

"Maybe this could work and I'm just overreacting."

But deep in the basement of her heart and soul she knew what had to be done. She had to let go of her baby boy, Moses. It felt like the weight of the world sat on her shoulders.

Her beloved people, God's children, were oppressed at the hand of a tyrant who saw them as nothing more than cheap labor. Despite the slavery that shackled her nation's feet, the Hebrews grew so much that it threatened their enemy. Frightened by the alarming rate of growth, Pharaoh quickly ordered the execution of all the Hebrews' newborn males. His orders were to drown these baby boys in the Nile River.

When God's people began to grow, the enemy grew nervous. It's also interesting that Pharaoh was more aware of their potential then even they were. The enemy knows your potential, perhaps better then you do. He knows what you're capable of and what could happen to his kingdom if you ever realized your greatness.

These unborn babies had an execution over their heads before they took one breath. It's no wonder that Satan attacks you before you ever discover what's within. He's banking that you will never realize your destiny. He hopes that preemptive strikes against your womanhood will silence your dreams all together.

Don't Lose your Lullaby

Jochebed was caught right in the middle of a national crisis. She knew her son's fate. She knew that a death sentence loomed over her womb. During a time when most couples are bubbling with anticipation, feeling for the baby's kicks and preparing for their new addition, Jochebed endured sleepless nights, tears and frustration. She already witnessed babies being stripped from their mother's arms only to be tossed into the river. Lullabies became loud cries as grieving mothers drank from the cup of misery.

Can you imagine what she must have felt?

Then, of course, there is the constant wrestling with the question, "Is it a boy or girl?" Everything in her fiber hoped for a girl. At least then she could finally wake up from her nightmare. Jochebed, like many women today, agonized over what she couldn't control. I wonder if you are worrying, stressing or losing sleep over an unforeseen situation in your life. Are you agonizing over the questions that you cannot answer? Jochebed was fortunate. While her emotions played tug-of-war, it didn't jeopardize her pregnancy.

However, you may not be so fortunate. Constant worry and stress can choke the destiny that God has placed within you. Wrap your arms around your joy. Don't give Satan a license to wreck your faith. Don't grieve about hollow threats or complain about your woes.

Sing your lullaby! Rejoice in spite of your circumstance. Speak life to your unborn dreams and promises. If you stop singing your lullaby, your hope will slowly evaporate. Like an unborn baby hears his mother's voice from inside the womb, the ears of your dream perk up every time you sing or speak faith. The power of life and death are in the tongue. Burn your complaint list and write your prayer list. Let your lullaby be heard!

Although Jochebed couldn't pick her situation, she was not powerless to change it. This is what you have to remember: Life isn't always going to be fair, but with God you have the ability to change your future.

Let Go and Let God

Destiny and deliverance grew in Jochebed's womb. Her unborn child was handpicked by God to deliver Israel out of bondage. Moses would be the one to stand before Pharaoh and command, "Let my people go!" He would become the great releaser of God's people. And yet, years before he would utter those words, his own mother had to "let him go."

You never know what your "let go" prepares you for. This is why as you grow in your faith, God will ask and require certain things from your life. Most, if not all the time, they are keepsakes of the heart and you often see no valid reason to let them go. But I urge you, whether small or large, let those things go. Letting go may bring you momentary pain or discomfort, but it will prepare a greater blessing further down the road.

God tests your willingness to "let go," He checks whether He can trust you with His calling and anointing. Jochebed never imagined that her "let go" would eventually "let go of her people." Her sacrifice not only saved her, but a whole nation. It allowed God to take full control of her destiny.

Isn't that what you want? As a woman, wife, or mother, don't you want God in control of your destiny and purpose? If so, don't be afraid to let go of the things He desires from you.

Give God the treasures you've buried in your heart. Trust that whatever he requires, he needs for his holy purposes. God doesn't owe you an explanation. He isn't obligated to reveal His secret plans. Just know and trust that He's working for your good.

As the breeze whisked through the brush and gently swirled around her legs, her mind took her back several days. She sat somberly inside her tent as she slowly weaved papyrus reeds into a basket. The more she weaved, the more unraveled her heart became. The more she coated the basket with sticky tar, the more unglued her life seemed.

Crafting this little ark would save her son's life. Yet a daunting paradox stood in the room. She pondered for a moment, "Why does doing something so right, feel so wrong? Why can't I just be happy about this?" On the verge of ripping her basket to pieces and refusing to continue, her motherly love kept her hands weaving.

Love compelled Jochebed to put her feelings, wants and wishes second. The gushing power of her love pushed her selfish desires aside. The red thread in most trials is to prove your love, not just your faith. Jochebed loved God enough to let go of her child, her dream. She also loved her child enough to let him go—because with her, his fate was sealed. The temptation to save what you have has always been an issue. But you have to understand that you can become the greatest obstacle to your own hopes.

Oftentimes, you get in the way you.

And while your motives may be pure, they undermine your own blessings. The widow of Sidon and her son (Ref. 1 Kings 17:7-24) had to let go of their last meager meal to feed a prophet. I don't blame her for first wanting to keep what little she had during one of the worst famines. She was so frail and thin that her bones begged for meat. No one is saying that your situation is easy or that you're not hungry for hope. However, if you learn to give what you have inside, God will exchange it for something that will feed you through the famine.

The widow of Sidon was just like her jar of oil and flour—empty. But when she gave what she couldn't live without, God blessed her with abundance. Just like Abraham tied Isaac to the altar and Hannah surrendered Samuel to the priesthood, God wants to know if you love Him more than your gifts. He wants to see if you're willing to sacrifice your dreams in exchange for Him.

Perhaps Jesus Christ knows this better than anyone. Shutting the door on His human feelings and concerns, Jesus allowed His body to be tied and nailed to a rugged Cross. Pushing aside every hint of selfish desire, Jesus surrendered His life to atone the sins of all humanity. Don't be alarmed. God isn't asking for your death, but rather your life. He isn't asking you to die, but to forsake all and live for Him.

Chapter 7

Your Dreams Won't Drown

The time had come.

This was the moment of truth for Jochebed. She couldn't turn back. So with one wet kiss to Moses' puckered little lips, she bent over and placed the basket in the river. Then with one last peek at this face, she nudged the floating cradle into the current and watched her precious son drift away. Her eyes swelled with tears and her face wrinkled with despair. The mother in her wanted to scream, but she squeezed her lips tight to not draw attention.

Taking a deep breath, she turned around and began what felt like the longest walk of her life.

Beneath the rubble of her broken heart was a resilient hope that everything would work out. Jochebed's dismay didn't shake her purpose. Everything was carefully planned out. A few days of surveillance and she knew when and where Pharaoh's daughter bathed in the river. Although her timing was strategic, it was God who whistled the wind and guided the basket towards the palace.

Several insights are striking at this point in the story. First, this woman teaches us that no matter how emotional you are about your situation, you still must plan and prepare. Don't let the riptide of feelings rob you of your divine moment. Pay attention to the promptings of the Holy Ghost. Listen to God's voice and be sensitive to His lead. He has arranged a royal touch for your dream. He has prepared a princess, a golden opportunity.

Of all the places Jochebed could have dropped off her child, she chose the exact site where other babies were executed. This seemed so illogical and self-contradictory to her mission. Naturally you would head in the opposite direction and avoid all contact with such a disturbing place.

But interwoven in the fabric of this story, we find another key insight: the same attack designed to drown Moses, God used to deliver him.

Why did God choose the Nile River as the turning point?

Because God always takes us back to the place where we gave up hope. He leads us back to a place of impossibility.

Not so we can relive the horror or shame, but so that we can see God's glory. At the same time, you come face to face with your fears.

Perhaps the main point is this: What Satan meant for evil, God meant for good.

The thick brush hid the basket as it floated down stream. Jochebed's eyes were hollow with hurt and her limbs were numb with shock. Each footprint in the marsh left behind the remnant of her motherhood.

"What kind of mother am I? Who would do what I just did?"

I imagine these questions broke into her mind like a burglar in the night. Yet an underflow of hope and faith filled her soul. Deep within she knew she did the right thing. She must have thought, "Where do I go from here? What's next?"

Meanwhile, the basket was now with Pharaoh's daughter. One glance at little Moses and her heart filled with love. Remember that an experience that brings you pain, will bring others relief. What made you cry will make someone smile again. What broke your heart will mend another. Your testimony will touch people you've never met or hoped to reach. When you let your dreams sail into the wind of God's will, you never know who or what will be affected.

This infant wasn't just a number or statistic in her father's holocaust, but a living, breathing child. If she reported her finding or simply turned a blind eye, her conscience would haunt her for the rest of her life.

Out of nowhere, the plot spins.

As the princess cradled the infant and pondered her options, little Miriam dashed towards her from a distance. By now the princess is puzzled, about to panic. The last thing she wants to do is create a scene.

With rosy cheeks and bated breath Miriam said, "Hey, I know this baby's nurse. If you want, I can go get her. She can nurture the child until he grows up a little." Without hesitation, the princess nodded in agreement.

The story suggests that Jochebed wasn't aware of her daughter's actions. It seems as though Miriam acted alone. However, if you look closer, you'll see God pulling the strings. When Miriam sprinted back to her mom and blurted the news, Jochebed couldn't believe her ears. Not only was she overjoyed about her chance to wean her child for several years, but the fact that her daughter played a key role. Because of Miriam's request, Jochebed got her child back!

Miriam is a picture of praise. She was the one who took the lead in the song of triumph after the passage of the Red Sea. The bible says that she grabbed a tambourine and gathered all the women to worship. Together they danced, shouted, sang, celebrated and glorified God. So, not only does Miriam represent praise, but more specifically, women who praise.

Having a spirit of praise and worship will spark new life in your dreams. If you can praise God when all hell seems to break loose and trouble is on every side, God will restore what you've lost. Praise is the link between you and your blessing. It will grant you favor and blessings that you weren't supposed to have. It will bring back your victory.

Praise and worship tugs on the heartstrings of God and woos His presence into your life. Whether you're in a pinch or enduring the darkest hour of your life, muster up some praise and worship. Do what feels unnatural, unnecessary and unwarranted. Praise the Lord for His goodness and mercy. Remember that your hope is still alive. Take into account that the river should have ruined you, but your baby—your hope, your dreams are still alive.

A Mother's Influence

"Yes, go," she answered. And the girl went and got the baby's mother. Pharaoh's daughter said to her, "Take this baby and nurse him for me, and I will pay you." So the woman took the baby and nursed him. (Exodus 2:8-9, NIV).

The more rare a commodity is, the more precious it is—especially time. Many consider time to be the most precious commodity. When distant relatives come to visit, the family attempts to make the most of their time together. And as you get a little older, you quickly realize that time is a gift.

Jochebed, posing as a nurse, embraced her baby again. The dream that she thought was gone forever, was now back in her arms. Everything was a bit of a blur. Her emotions were stretched in every direction. She walked home with the baby she kissed goodbye just moments ago.

"Somebody pinch me," she thought in disbelief.

This was all too surreal, too bizarre. Warm fresh tears began to flow as she snuggled his tiny body against her chest. After a sigh of relief, she suddenly felt alive again. Not to be seen, she swaddled his body and tucked him tight into her garments. Not wanting to draw attention to herself, she wiped her tears, fixed her hair and composed herself. Yet, under her breath, she praised God and uttered tender words of thanksgiving.

Coupled with her joy was also a glaring foresight. The clock began ticking the moment she walked away from the princess. As surprised as she was about this gift, she knew it was temporary. Someday soon she would again stroll down that tearstained path to the palace and hand over her child. Perhaps most mothers would squeeze lemons and charge God with injustice. Many mothers might see this as a teaser, not a blessing. But Jochebed had an attitude of gratitude. So, she did the wise thing; she made every moment count.

Knowing that her days with Moses were numbered, she spared no opportunity to wean, instruct, train and cherish. She knew she was parenting on barrowed time. Here's the point you need to remember: Jochebed already gave her child away.

She already dedicated him to God. Unlike before that somber day at the river, she knew that she didn't own child, but God did. This time, she had a spiritual understanding about whom she was raising.

After the events on Mount Moriah, Abraham saw Isaac in a different light. He never viewed him the same again. The same was true for Jochebed and is also true for you today. When God returns your surrendered dreams, you feel humbled, honored, undeserving, and a heightened sense of responsibility. You are no longer controlling your possessions, but managing what belongs to God.

Treat your blessings, dreams, desires, miracles and especially your children as gifts from God. Maximize your time. If you're a mother, what I'm about to share is vital. There are three things that Moses would never forget in those few tender years. Likewise, you have three important blessings to pass on to your children.

1. Your Voice

From the time Jochebed knew she was pregnant until the final walk towards Pharaoh's palace, she never stopped speaking to him. Her voice was inside of him. Even when he became a man, he never forgot his mother's voice. It was a reminder of who he was and where he came from. Your voice is one of the greatest imprints you can leave on your children. Even when they are grown, they will still hear your voice in their hearts. What a privilege you have! Be wise with your words. They can either build up or tear down. If your voice is negative, your words will sear deep into your child's heart.

Let your voice reinforce your child's purpose and character. No matter how loud trials and tragedies become, your child will always hear your voice whispering through.

2. *Your Values*

Moses spent his most impressionable years in an immoral and godless environment. Under the roof of Pharaoh, he was exposed to multiple gods, ideologies and customs. Yet in the midst of that atmosphere, he never forgot Jochebed's values and spiritual center.

As a boy, she likely rehearsed his distinct identity and made sure he knew how special he was. "Moses, you're not an Egyptian. You're a Hebrew—chosen by God." Those words echoed in his heart and always reminded him that he wasn't like his adopted family. When Moses was forty-years-old, he refused to be labeled as an Egyptian. (Ref. Hebrews 11:24-25)

Moses knew that he belonged to a different family and heritage. Pass down your values to your children. Never leave your beliefs to assumption. Clarify your morals and Christian principles; so that wherever your children find themselves, they'll remember that they belong to God's family.

3. Your Vision

Give your children wings. Pour purpose into their lives by defining their identity and allowing them to dream big. Prepare them for flight, the opportunity to soar to latitudes that you never reached. As unappealing as Pharaoh's palace was to Jochebed, she knew that it was the place where God would raise Moses up. The palace would actually position Moses for his destiny as Israel's deliverer.

Where are you pointing your children?

Where have you launched them?

Psalm 127:4 says, *"Like arrows in the hand of a warrior, So are the children of one's youth."* Arrows are useless if they are not pointed at a target. No matter how hard you pull back the bow, the arrow won't hit anything significant unless it's aimed at a target. You could be pushing your kids hard and not see any results because they are not being aimed correctly. It's time to set a clear vision for their lives.

Drawn Out

When the child grew older, she took him to Pharaoh's daughter and he became her son. She named him Moses, saying, "I drew him out of the water" (Exodus 2:10, NIV).

The moon hung low and the stars glistened like diamonds on black velvet. The warm sand began to chill under the desert breeze. Stillness swept across the village and the whole world seemed to be fast asleep. However, there was one mother who couldn't rest. After tossing and turning for several hours, Jochebed left her bed and curled up next to Moses. With the back of her fingers she caressed his delicate cheeks and watched him breathe. Absorbing every detail, she couldn't untangle the knot of emotions in her heart.

Tomorrow was the day that she would hand over her dream, Moses, back to Pharaoh's daughter.

The morning haze rolled back as the sun peaked over the crest of the desert. After some breakfast, a prayer, and final instructions, mother and son began their walk towards the palace. This was all too familiar for her. It felt like déjà vu, a flashback to her first walk along the Nile River. Both walks seemed to have sanded down the rough edges in her heart and smoothed out her perspective.

In contrast, this day couldn't be more different. Jochebed wasn't re-surrendering her child. Every day Moses lived with her, he was already surrendered to a greater cause. Instead of Jochebed fighting to let go, Moses was now old enough to sense what was happening. As any child would, he probably resisted. No amount of preparation can remove a child's instinct to cling to his mother. I imagine a scream and dirty tears cascading down Moses' face as they pulled him away from Jochebed. Although she surrendered him five years before, it didn't freeze the pain she felt in that moment.

With a quivered kiss and a tight hug she said goodbye to Moses for the second time.

Just like before, she turned around and walked home. Her arms were empty, but her spirit was full. Her faith in God was resolute and solid. She knew that this special child would rise up one day and set her and all of Israel free by the power of God.

Pharaoh's daughter gave Moses his name, which means "drawn out." Moses represents everything that God wants to "draw out" from your life. He has already placed the deliverance and dream inside of you.

There is overflowing joy for the woman who embraces the attitude and spirit of Jochebed. Regardless of what you're battling with, there is a sweet surrender that God is looking for. The Lord is preparing you for something that goes beyond where you've been. Your children, your community and world desperately need the gift that God has placed inside of you.

Chapter 8

Cultivating Courage

As a mother, Jochebed's heart was broken. But one thing that didn't break was her courage. Without it, she would have never made it to the Nile River or back to Pharaoh's palace. Her legs would have given out halfway. Yet beneath the salty tears of pain was a resilient heart, unbreakable courage to do the right thing. She refused to give in to the pressures of her enemy.

Perhaps you've heard the saying before; courage is not the absence of fear, but the will to act in spite of it. Did Jochebed ever get scared? There's no reason to believe she didn't. Even the toughest moms would buckle under that weight of pressure. Yet, she remained poised.

Helen Keller once said, "We could never learn to be brave and patient if there were only joy in the world." How true that is. Heroes are born in adversity, not tranquility.

The next time you feel afraid to step out into God's will and purpose for your life, you'll want to remember these pair of principles:

Principle One: *Embrace Risks, Not the Ordinary*
No matter how much faith Jochebed had, she still took a risk. She put everything on the line—including her reputation. What would other mothers think if they discovered Jochebed's secret? How would they feel knowing that her baby escaped the execution, and theirs didn't? I presume that a certain level of animosity bubbled up within the community of despaired mothers—whose arms were empty. It's likely that a subculture formed, an informal support group of mothers who lost their baby boys in the Nile.

Expectant mothers in the neighborhood knew who was pregnant. After the babies were killed, the nightmare had only begun. Surely they pondered and chatted among themselves.

"Hey, haven't you noticed that there's something different about Jochebed?"

"What do you mean?"

"Well, she seems rather composed, almost happier since

our baby boys drowned. She's carrying on as though nothing has happened. She hasn't even opened up once to share her feelings."

"Now that you mention it, she has been acting a little strange."

I imagine that when the secret became public and other childless mothers learned that Jochebed still had her son, there was some unavoidable tension. Soon she was singled out, because now it seemed she didn't have much in common with her peers.

Her faith and purpose drove a wedge between her and her friends. I can't speak for those other women. I can only assume that many didn't think her acquittal was fair. I'm sure some harbored no ill feelings. But my gut tells me that not everyone was happy for her. Not everyone could have possibly grasped the gravity of her calling. Not everyone would have appreciated or celebrated her personal victory.

You'll find that true purpose and courage will often divide you from people and things that you once related with. Courage oftentimes puts you on an island of hope. Your old friends may not completely understand your newfound joy. Certain people view your blessing with contempt. They don't think it's fair that you've been blessed in an area where they've been cursed. And although they won't admit it, they want your secret, your strategy.

Being a risk-taker always creates conflict with the ordinary. But nothing great ever happens when we sit back and accept the status quo. Jochebed demonstrated a courageous spirit when she listened to the voice of God and surrendered her child.

Embrace risks and never accept the ordinary. After her experience at the Nile River and with the Egyptian princess, Jochebed was a different woman. Everything changed. She had an experience that demanded a fresh perspective and a new lifestyle.

Principle Two: *Embrace Reality, Not the Outcome*

Denying a problem only fertilizes it. Jochebed never once denied her reality, which was—a death sentence had been ordered for her unborn son. This was a constant thought. She knew the threat was real. She just didn't accept the outcome. One truth you must capture about faith is that it's not a denial of reality, but an appeal.

When an ill person says, "I'm healed", she isn't denying the reality of her condition, she's declaring an unseen fact— which is, her sickness won't win. Hebrews 11:1 says, "Faith is the substance of things hoped for, the evidence of things not yet seen."

Denial has no positive value. To pretend that everything is fine when things are a mess isn't faith. Acting as though nothing is wrong when there is an obvious problem doesn't solve anything. Jochebed didn't ignore the threat, she counteracted. That's what courage is all about. It's not about turning a blind-eye, but envisioning your victory.

Was Jochebed scared?

Was her heart a blender of emotions?

If she was human (which she was), the answer is "yes".

Jochebed wasn't superwoman. She didn't have any superhuman strengths or emotions of steel. She had red blood pumping through her veins just like you. Yet, she overcame the odds because her belief in God was greater than her circumstance.

Courage is not about agreeing with the present reality, but with the end results. No matter what odds have stacked up against you, have the courage to move forward. Despite your situation, trust in God's sovereign will and purpose for your life. Dare to believe God at His word. Dare to be different.

Jochebed refused to be another statistic. She didn't deny her situation—she confronted it. She said "no" to Pharaoh, "no" to death. I wonder if in your mind, or out loud, you can say "NO"? If there are some threats looming over you, confront them. Declare God's word and believe what it says. You are more than a conqueror!

The length of Jochebed's story pales in comparison to the other women I've written about in this book. On that note, however, her legacy is unmatched. It's amazing how many lessons you can learn from such a short story. If we could travel back in time and interview her, I think she would have some priceless pearls of wisdom. I would imagine that one of her pearls for life would be: Never underestimate the power of one decision.

One decision literally turned Jochebed's entire life around. She chose to trust God by letting go of her most prized possession—her child. Perhaps you are just one decision away from a breakthrough in your life. One small act of courage could alter the course of your destiny.

Chapter 9

Unexpected Delays

How long would you wait for God's promises? One year? Five years? If you asked Sarah that question, she would probably answer, "a lifetime." Two facts come to mind when I think about Sarah. The first is that Sarah was Abraham's wife. Secondly, Sarah is the mother to the nation of Israel. Maybe you're thinking, "Wow, this woman is something else. How awesome and wonderful it must have been to be Sarah."

Sarah was blessed. And her mark on history is deeply imprinted—not only in history, but in the hearts of all those who worship the one true God.

However, as special as she was, Sarah had many learning experiences about life, faith and family. Being married to the father of faith was no glamorous position to be in. Sarah was often forced into situations that she had no control over.

In addition to that, Sarah wasn't your cookie-cutter Old Testament woman. Not that one actually existed. But if there were such a group, she would be in a category all to herself. To put it plainly, Sarah had some shrew moments, some episodes of bad behavior, manipulation, and even some cruelty. She had streaks of impatience, jealousy and belligerence. Not to mention her natural ability to throw a fit at the worst of times. This woman had all the symptoms of a get-what-I-want when-I-want kind of woman.

Wait…are we still talking about Sarah—mother of Isaac, grandmother of Jacob? In fact, we are. I suggest a cold drink, because these pages about to heat up.

When your Glass Slipper Breaks

The Bible gives us some clues about Sarah's personality that if you don't catch them, you won't fully understand the significance of her destiny. One overlooked clue is that her birth name was actually Sarai, later to be changed to Sarah. That change came at a high price. There's more to come on that. However, the name Sarai means "my princess".

Sounds harmless I guess. After all, it's just a name.

Well, not really.

In Old Testament times, names meant everything. They represented who a person was and many times embodied their character. In Sarah's case, she actually wasn't a "princess" in any kingdom or monarchy. Nor did she come from any royal bloodlines. With all due respect, Sarah started out as just a common girl.

The point is this; Sarah was raised with the idea that she was a princess—not literally, but idealistically. So naturally, she became an idealist, a person who sees things as they might or should be, rather than as they are. In case you're wondering, idealism and faith are entirely different. Idealism denies reality, while faith defies reality.

Adding to her name, she was also beautiful in appearance. Even at the age of sixty-five years old, Sarah was noted for her physical beauty. At sixty-five she could still turn heads, enough that kings and high-powered men took notice.

Problems await women who were raised in a what-I-want, when-I-want environment. Without being prepared for real life, adulthood is a collision course of ideals verses reality. Life is not a fairytale. No matter how many times you've watched Cinderella slip into her glass slippers, or no matter how many romance novels you've read, what you face everyday is a far cry from "happily ever after". This is not to say that your story won't end well, especially when God writes your script. However, unless you're prepared to deal with life's ups and downs, diverse personalities and unforeseen setbacks, you may find yourself swimming upstream.

Sarah started off somewhat on the wrong foot. Her name alone sends a clear message about her attitude towards life—and dare I say she had symptoms of a typical prima donna. Whenever you see a combination of special treatment, status, natural beauty and appeal in a woman, there is a greater vulnerability to this attitude.

"Prima donna" is Italian for "first lady", and was used to designate the leading female singer in opera houses. Prima donnas were often viewed as being vain, self-centered and difficult to work with. Unfortunately their talents were indispensable. Selfish behavior and high-maintenance was the hidden price the opera house had to pay in order to have star appeal.

My goal is not to classify Sarah as some pampered diva with an over-the-top personality. Her good qualities outweighed the bad, or else we wouldn't be talking about her today. God obviously saw something in her that he wanted, something he could use. Yet, I simply cannot skim over the reality that Sarah had plenty of personal pitfalls to overcome. A lot of maturity had to take place for her to realize her dreams. The greatest part of that maturity involved something that she wanted desperately, but couldn't have—a baby.

Genesis 15:5 says, *"He took him outside and said, "Look up at the heavens and count the stars—if indeed you can count them." Then he said to him, "So shall your offspring be."*

Then we read in Genesis 16:1, *"Now Sarai, Abram's wife, had borne him no children..."*

Sarah's glass slipper broke.

Better yet, her world came crashing down when she realized she wasn't getting pregnant. Possibly for the first time, she felt vulnerable and scared. It's safe to say a sense of inadequacy began to gnaw away at her heart, one bite at a time. Everything that she had hoped for, dreamed about, came to a screeching halt. Now, instead of feeling like a princess, she felt like less of a woman.

Sarah's upbringing certainly didn't prepare her for this trial. But to her defense, such circumstances can't always be prepared for. No one prepares for failure or tragedy. We simply learn to cope with the worst and hope for the best. Sarah had a collision with reality. The hardest part was not that she couldn't conceive and have children. As difficult as that was, there were cultural solutions that could jumpstart her family. Adoption and surrogate motherhood were accepted answers to infertility.

The true problem here was that her husband received a prophecy about having children. In fact, a whole nation was to come from her and Abraham. All of the sudden, the pressure is on.

"If God has called me to be a mother...why can't I have children?"

"If I'm supposed to be this special woman, why do I feel so insecure and inadequate?"

"What's wrong with me?"

Certainly these questions festered on in her mind. Have you ever fought with questions like these? Have you ever struggled with your own femininity? Have you ever questioned your calling?

If so, you're not alone. Most women encounter a time in life when the class slipper cracks, and the ideals of life pop like a bloated balloon. Maybe you're at that junction right now. Allow the Holy Spirit to calm your fears today. Everything you're feeling and struggling with is preparing you—maturing your faith to receive what God has in store.

Dealing with Unexpected Delays

I'll admit that one of the toughest things to do is wait—especially when you're en route to a destination. For a simple illustration, look no further than airline transportation. It can be a frustrating experience, to arrive at the airport, only to learn that your particular flight has been delayed. By this time, you might have already passed through the security checkpoint, so leaving and coming back is out of the question. You woke up early, grabbed a quick bite, maneuvered through rush-hour traffic, spilled a little coffee, hauled your suitcases to the baggage check-in, took off your shoes for security, whisked down the terminal, only to hear the airline announce that your flight will be delayed at least an hour.

Even though your body and mind are in full swing, ready to travel, your schedule is delayed and your plans are put on hold. It's an uncomfortable feeling to have the brakes slammed on your progress. You look like a traveler, but you're not going anywhere. Now, it's one thing for this to happen in your hometown airport. There is a sense of security knowing that you're still minutes from home, and if things get worse, you can always reschedule. The worst feeling is, however, when you're stuck between two destinations and your layover becomes an overnighter. You're not at home, and you're not at your destination. You're delayed in transit.

Life itself is full of unexpected delays. There are times when you feel ready to leap into an area of ministry or business, only to learn that your progress is delayed. There are times when you're ready to start a family, only to realize that you're unable to have children. Sarah could relate. Having waved goodbye to her hometown, she followed her husband—only to discover everything she hoped to gain out of this decision was delayed.

Sarah's dreams lost momentum when she was faced with some unexpected delays. Instead of enjoying her promise child, she had to sit tight, and wait for her moment to come.

The hardest thing for Sarah to do was wait. Perhaps it was her class slipper syndrome or simply wanting to avoid embarrassment. Either way, waiting was not her ideal situation. She hadn't prepared to wait. This evidentially would be her defining test of character and faith. It's funny how God chooses to test your areas of weakness, not strengths. However, He does this so that you can learn, grow and mature into your promise. This way, your promise will be preserved.

You cannot become who God wants you to become with your old mentality, habits and issues. Your old lifestyle cannot support the depth of your new destiny. If God were to pour a new promise into your old self, the whole thing would fall apart. Jesus once elaborated on this issue. *"And no one puts new wine into old wineskins; or else the new wine will burst the wineskins and be spilled, and the wineskins will be ruined. But new wine must be put into new wineskins, and both are preserved"* (Luke 5:37-38).

Wineskins were simply containers made from animal hide, for the purpose of storing wine. When a wineskin got old, it would gradually lose its elasticity. If you were to pour new wine into an old wineskin, the skin would split and burst because of the intense fermentation. In order for new wine to ferment properly, it must be poured into new skins. The old wineskin represents your old mentality. The new wine represents God's new promise for your life. If God pours his new promise into your old mentality, you won't be prepared to receive it.

Sarah still had layers of old wineskins on her heart and mind. Even though God had promised her a son, she wasn't ready to receive and nurture a blessing of this scale. Sarah had a lot of growing up to do. Her faith needed refining before she would ever become the woman we know today. Even though she was probably in her sixties, she still needed to grow up.

You see, no matter how great your potential is—God won't hand you a blessing you're not ready for. He knows that if he pours into your old mentality or womanhood, it will burst out and everything you hoped for will be spoiled. So, to prepare you, God announces your progress is being delayed. This is where your buried issues will surface and unfinished business will come to light. It's in the waiting room where God sees what kind of woman you are, and how much refining is necessary.

The waiting room of unexpected delays and prolonged progress will tell God exactly where your attitude is. God uses delays to check your spiritual temperature and how well you adapt to uncertainty. Most of all, he's testing your faith to see if you'll trust him through desperate times. This is where patience comes in.

Patience is waiting with the right heart. The Psalmist David penned, *"Be still before the LORD and wait patiently for him..."* (Psalm 37:7). True patience isn't when someone waits, yet complains and nags the entire time. It isn't just the time you spend waiting, it's the attitude you have while you wait. For instance, even though the Israelites waited to enter the Promised Land, a whole generation could not enter because of "how" they waited. This is also the reason why God doesn't bless certain people who are waiting for an answer. If your heart is angry with God, or bitter about the process, your character needs polishing.

The other side of patience is tolerance when dealing with irritating or difficult people. It might mean biting your tongue or giving someone a second chance. God is also watching how you deal with those around you, including your husband, children, friends and co-workers.

Unexpected delays drove Sarah to the edge. As you'll see, instead of bearing down and waiting patiently on God, she pressed the panic button.

Chapter 10

Panic Room

In the film, *Panic Room*, Meg Altman (played by Jodie Foster), and her daughter Sarah (Kristen Stewart), find themselves in a race against time and two greedy burglars who become increasingly agitated and violent. The film focuses on what's called a "panic room". A panic room is basically a protected room that is secretly located in some luxury homes. On the mother and daughter's first night in their new home, two thieves broke in, hoping to snatch three-million-dollars in bearer bonds that were left by the previous owner. The mother and daughter used the panic room to hide and protect themselves until the police arrived. The movie is quite a thriller and definitely keeps you on the edge of your seat.

I'm no film critic, so the reason I mention this movie is to shine light on the panic rooms that women often run to in times of trouble and waiting. Although the movie's panic room offered "protection" and not more "panic", it breaks the ice on how easy it is to panic when hopes are dim.

Sarah panicked.

She could hear her biological clock ticking. No child. No signs of pregnancy. Little by little, Sarah became a difficult woman to live with. She was frustrated with herself — unhappy with how things were going.

Abraham noticed and I'm sure he tried to cheer her up.

Let's talk little bit about Abraham, not the Patriarch, but the husband. The hardest thing for a husband to do is approach his wife about her aggravation. The last thing Abraham wanted was an argument. Because he knew that no matter he said, he couldn't change her feelings. Plus, the wrong tone or slight misunderstanding could do more harm then help.

However, he couldn't deny the obvious. He knew exactly why Sarah was bothered these days — still no baby. In fact, I'm sure Abraham even felt partly to blame for her feelings. He was the one who uprooted her life and convinced her to buy into this dream. He was the one who sold the idea and gave her hope. To think that Abraham was completely detached from Sarah's emotions is quite untrue. He could read her body language. He could sense that she was feeling the heat, the pressure. She didn't feel like something was wrong with the plan, but that something was wrong with her. Maybe she wasn't the woman she thought she was. Maybe she overestimated herself. As most women would, she took it personal.

I wouldn't doubt that the most troubling thing for Abraham was not that his wife was becoming cold with him, but even with God.

So Sarai said to Abram, "See now, the LORD has restrained me from bearing children…" (Genesis 16:2a)

At face value, this statement may seem simple or unrevealing. But if you listening closely, you'll hear that Sarah is venting. This is the boiling point in her heart—a final complaint and abandonment of responsibility.

Sarah was essentially saying…

"Okay Abraham, this is it. I've taken all I can and am ready to pull the plug on this thing. God himself must not want me to give birth. I've waited. I clung to whatever shred of hope there was. But I'm tired of pretending that things are good. I feel like God is playing with my emotions. One moment I'm excited, the next moment you have to scrape my heart off the floor with a spatula. I feel like the punch line of a joke. I'm not laughing anymore. God has prevented me...better yet, restrained me from getting pregnant. This is where I draw the line. Game over."

Sarah was entangled in a web of emotions. She lost all patience. She found herself in a place where you might be today—at your wits end. But here's where things went from bad to worse. The easiest thing to believe is that Sarah lost grip of her faith, or that she didn't have any faith. However, if Sarah had a lack of faith, she would have never bought into the promise. Sure, we can't deny the role of faith in receiving her child. God was precisely interested in Sarah's total trust. That was the glue that kept this whole plan together.

What made Sarah tense was her lack of gratitude. She was so consumed over what she didn't have, that she nearly ruined what she did have.

I wonder if you can relate?

Have you become so frustrated with one of your child's poor decisions that you neglected to celebrate your other children? Have you become so tense about losing your childhood dream that you haven't thanked God for the roof over your head? Have you become so jealous of another woman's success that you haven't appreciated yours? Have you become so disappointed with your husband's negative qualities that you cease to enjoy his positive qualities? Have you focused too much on where you wish to be, rather than praise God for where you are now? Have worried too much about what you've lost, as opposed to what you've gained?

Believe me, I know these are hard questions. But this is a wake up call—an alarm to your soul. It's possible that you are about to lose a valuable relationship, a career or a ministry. If these pages are starting to feel hot, it's because God is trying to send you message.

Sarah allowed herself to lose total control of her emotions and actions. Her frustration got the best of her. And the truth is, your frustration will get the best of you too. Your marriage could suffer. Your kids could withdraw from you. You may find yourself unable to smile, unable to be yourself.

Perhaps you think no one notices that you're unhappy. But they do. And like Abraham, maybe they just don't want to further upset you. They don't want to compound the situation. They know that if they bring it up, it will only upset you, ruin your appetite, or silence you for the evening.

Overcoming this kind of frustration begins with gratitude. Let me give you three gifts to start appreciating, three ways to get out of the panic room of ungratefulness.

1. The Gift of Life

I know this one sounds simple. But far too often we neglect to appreciate the gift of life. Life is so precious, so dear; we must thank God for breathing the breath of life into our lungs and giving us health. When you appreciate being alive, it takes you to the core of what life is really all about. This is why most people who have had near death experiences or have recovered from fatal illnesses have a much simpler, purer appreciation for life. They are grateful for another day because they kissed eternity. Surely it doesn't take a brush with death to respect the gift of life.

2. The Gift of Small Things

As someone once said, "stop and smell the roses." When was the last time you did just that? Life can be so busy, stressful at times that you could miss out on some small treasures. In your busyness, focusing all your attention on what you don't have, you miss out on the simple blessings around you. Take time to notice and appreciate the ordinary, the seemingly mundane things. Don't take small blessings for granted. What we consider ordinary benefits are considered luxuries in many parts of the world. Be thankful for the little things.

3. The Gift of God

Jesus once told a woman from Samaria, *"If you knew the gift of God, and who it is who says to you, 'Give Me a drink,' you would have asked Him, and He would have given you living water"* (John 4:10). Let's not overlook the greatest gift of all—Jesus Christ, our Lord and Savior. Appreciate the fact that you have God in your life. Consider where you would be without Him, without His grace, His mercy, His love. Maybe it's time to thank God again for the gift of salvation, the fact that you were once doomed, but are now forgiven. Be ever more grateful that Jesus Christ, God manifested in flesh, died on the cross for your sins.

When Sarah panicked, it became easier to compromise her destiny. Not even Abraham could see Sarah's next move.

When Insecurity Meets Uncertainty

"Please, go in to my maid; perhaps I shall obtain children by her."
And Abram heeded the voice of Sarai. (Genesis 16:2b)

Sarah was at the peak of her impatience. In her mind, she had waited long enough. Her faith was stunted, and each day gave birth to fresh worries. Where was God? When was this "promise child" going to come? These questions kept her up at night. This child represented far more than just having a family, but a nation. And she felt like she was the only thing standing between her promise.

Sarah's plan was to use her maidservant Hagar as a surrogate mother. Once the child was born, Sarah would assume the role of mother. This way, her and Abraham would have the son they were promised. The waiting would end. The family tree would be complete and everyone lives happily ever after.

Well, not quite.

There were two fundamental problems with Sarah's plan, 1) Sarah wasn't the mother and 2) the child wasn't the promise.

Surrogacy wasn't a new idea. In fact, Sarah would not have suggested it unless it was an acceptable practice. But this idea of swapping wives to produce a child bypassed God's will. Hagar had nothing to do with the promise. God never considered her an option or an alterative, because He knew that his plan wouldn't fail.

Sadly, she slowly began to count herself out. This mindset is a dream killer, a destiny destroyer. Sarah starting thinking that maybe this promise wasn't really about her—that perhaps she wasn't as important as originally thought. Why else would Sarah introduce an idea, such as using her maid for a surrogate mother, unless she doubted her own significance? At some point, she began to question her own purpose—even more so, her own relevance.

Have you ever second-guessed yourself? Have you doubted your calling, your abilities, your strength, your identity, or perhaps your value? Sarah did. She found herself questioning everything, including her own importance in God's plan.

You must believe that YOU MATTER. You cannot be replaced like a tire on a car, or a button on a blouse. You are too important, too distinct, and too special to drop out of being you. It's not good enough for your husband to believe in you, or even your parents. You have to believe in you. You have to know how great you are, and what you're capable of accomplishing.

Sarah was married to the man of the century, and it had no bearing on her self-worth. As great as Abraham was, she had to believe she was equally great. She had to be convinced of her own legacy.

Every woman has insecurities, reasons to feel unsure about herself. Below, I've listed some issues associated with insecurity:

- Anxiety
- Confusion
- Feeling Defenseless
- Doubt
- Embarrassment
- Hesitation
- Incompetence
- Indecision
- Instability

Do any of these words describe an area in your life? What types of circumstances tend to bring out these insecurities? You have to remember that this is simply part of being human. You are not weak, or any less of a woman, because you harbor these feelings. Additionally, God doesn't always erase these insecurities. He wants to help us master them, and to depend on the Holy Spirit.

At this point, Sarah has excluded herself from the plans and has now introduced a new plan—plan B.

This new plan compromised her marriage. There was no such thing as an embryonic transfer in those days. That meant the only way Hagar could become pregnant is if Abraham had sexual relations with her. This is where things spin out of control.

Sarah essentially gave her husband the license to sleep with Hagar and violate the sanctity of their relationship. She didn't think her decision through. But rather, she became impulsive and did what she had to do...to get what she wanted. Sarah didn't consider the repercussions of her scheme—the toll it would take on her family, her marriage. She was blinded with ambition and lost sight of the things that really mattered.

Sarah didn't think hard enough about who would get hurt, who would suffer. This decision wasn't even about

Abraham or God's plan. It was all about Sarah. It was a selfish move masked with good intentions.

I wonder, can you relate in any way, shape or form? Have you ever made a decision without counting the cost? Without considering who would be hurt, or how long it would take to pick up the broken pieces? Have you ever been blinded with ambition, and even tried to put God's name on it to justify your decision? Maybe Sarah had conversations with God that were entirely one-sided. Just because you tell God your plans, doesn't mean he approves.

Sarah may have looked like a woman who had everything under control. But looks can be deceiving. Sarah had completely lost control of her emotions and better judgment.

Timing is Everything

As I mentioned, this was no longer about a nation, a promise, or God's will. This was purely about Sarah. It had Sarah's name written all over it. It was about a princess-minded woman who wasn't getting what she wanted, when she wanted it. So, she went to great lengths, even pushing her husband into another woman's arms, to satisfy her selfish whims.

This exact scenario happens today. A modern woman can become so engulfed in a career, a venture, or even a ministry, that she pushes her husband into the arms of another. It could be the arms of a woman, a relationship, a hobby, or a habit—anything that shows him attention. Perhaps you need to yourself, "Am I pursuing something at the cost of my marriage or family?" Time and again we see people, not just women, who sacrifice what they need, for they want.

Sarah did just that. She compromised what she needed (a loving husband and an intact home), for what she wanted. And, it didn't matter that what she wanted was ultimately good. What mattered was that she was willing to put her most valuable relationships on the line to obtain it.

What's the lesson here?

The right thing, at the wrong time, is the wrong thing.

That can be a painful lesson to learn. Sometimes in our ambition to fulfill a dream, we hurt people we love along the way. In that case, the right thing, at the wrong time, is the wrong thing. In your pursuit of a ministry (honorable as it is), if people get stepped on and abandoned in the process, the right thing, at the wrong time, is the wrong thing. If you're a single mother wanting a husband, but doing so means even less "mom time" and nurturing, well...I think you know what I'm going to say.

Timing is one of the most valuable lessons I've learned in my life. You cannot force God's hand. He will move when he's good and ready. Any attempt to expedite the process creates huge risks—or as in Sarah's case, huge consequences.

Men don't get a pass either. Abraham could have rejected the idea. However, the problem didn't start with him. It started with Sarah. Later on, Sarah tried throwing the entire situation in Abraham's face, hoping to split the guilt in half. According to Genesis 16:5, Sarah basically blamed Abraham for how things turned out.

But his response was swift..."Indeed your maid is in your hand; do to her as you please." In other words, "Sarah, this was your idea, your doing. I can't fix it for you. You have to take responsibility for your actions." That's not what she wanted to hear, but definitely what she needed to hear. Sarah's ambitions were out of control. And everyone around her had to walk on eggshells, including her husband.

I understand Sarah took things to the extreme. And her attitude affected the whole house. As a woman, you have great influence in your home. Your mood actually sets the mood in the home. You are the emotional thermostat in your family. As the old saying goes, "If momma's not happy, nobody's happy."

Maybe I'm treading on thin ice with my insights. But unless women look honestly at Sarah's actions, they won't know how to deal with their own emotions and womanhood. Sarah single-handedly changed the environment of her family. That's how much power you have dear woman. Even if your kids are grown and out of the nest, your attitude and actions influence the entire family—large or small.

Chapter 11

Conquering your Insecurities

Sarah's insecurities began to get the best of her. In the wake of her poor choices, she now had to deal with another problem—Hagar—who was merely a pawn in her plan. Hagar was Sarah's maid. Her primary responsibility was to serve and assist Sarah with all of her daily needs. Anything Sarah needed help with, Hagar was there. She depended on her. So when Sarah proposed that Abraham have sexual relations with Hagar, she was basically swapping roles. Hagar acted as the wife, the lead role, and Sarah acted as the servant, the supporting role.

Abraham listened to Sarah and slept with Hagar. Then just as she planned, Hagar became pregnant. This is when things really began to go sour for Sarah. Now, there is contempt, bad blood between Sarah and Hagar. The same plan that brought these women together...drove them apart.

Genesis 16:4 says, *"So he went in to Hagar, and she conceived. And when she saw that she had conceived, her mistress became despised in her eyes"*. Once Hagar became pregnant, she treated Sarah with scorn. Sarah was blindsided by this problem. She had no clue that halfway through her scheme, her accomplice would turn on her—making her to feel like an outcast in her own home.

This is a classic example of what happens when two insecure women face off. Sarah was insecure for devising this plan. Hagar was insecure for parading her childbearing abilities. Hagar allowed herself to become proud and sassy. What little advantage she had—she abused. Sarah became jealous and cruel.

Neither woman was comfortable in her own skin. This was a recipe for disaster. If they had spent the same amount of time and energy celebrating who they were as individual women, they would have never felt the urge to compete.

Women compete for attention and status because they want significance. Seeing Hagar's pregnant belly grow everyday was a constant reminder of what Sarah lacked—a child. On the flip side, when Hagar saw how much Abraham adored Sarah it was a constant reminder of she lacked—a healthy marriage. Both wanted to feel significant and valuable, which they already were in God's eyes.

How to Conquer your Insecurities

As you can probably tell, this isn't your traditional "women of the bible" story. I deliberately avoided the usual hallmarks in Sarah's life, because my goal is to show you the human side of her. It's too easy to categorize all of her mistakes and insecurities as a "lack of faith" or "doubt". That, in my humble opinion, is the religious answer. The truth is, like Sarah, our reasons for not experiencing God's blessings go much deeper.

Sarah's biggest struggle wasn't just doubt, but her insecurities. She constantly played tug-of-war with her emotions and fears. It took many hard lessons for her to grow into the woman we all admire and respect today. I would like to pour a fresh supply of hope for dealing with insecurities. To accomplish that, let me suggest five principles to live by:

Principle One: Deepen your Prayer Life

Deepening your relationship with God is such a vital part of mastering your insecurities. So often the bible shines the light on characters that were unpolished, yet they reached out for God. Nearly all of life's struggles can be hashed out on your knees. Of course, I'm talking about prayer. When you pray, you afford God the opportunity to probe your heart and strengthen your spirit. Prayer is a place where you can pour out your feelings, frustrations and concerns. It's a place where you can cry out for help and connect with God.

What better way to deal with your insecurities then by linking up with the most secure source? Nothing is as secure, stable and strong as the Lord Jesus Christ. Paul said, "I can do all things through who strengthens me" (Phil. 4:13). His strength is unbreakable.

Prayer is the key to knowing God and receiving spiritual nourishment. It is the ultimate lifeline to your spirit. The more time you spend in prayer, the more God can speak to you, guide you, shape you, and reinforce his will in your life. Prayer allows your spirit to talk with God and release all of your heart's hidden issues.

1 John 5:14-15 reveals, *"Now this is the confidence that we have in Him, that if we ask anything according to His will, He hears us. And if we know that He hears us, whatever we ask, we know that we have the petitions that we have asked of Him."*

When you pray, God hears you. Whatever you ask of him, he will do according to his will. Mastering your insecurities starts with prayer. It starts with relating to the One who has an undefeated record, the One who is never insecure.

When Moses asked God, "what shall I say to the children of Israel when they ask who sent me?" God told him to say, "I AM has sent me to you" (Ref. Exodus 3). Now that's what I call being secure about who are you! God basically said, "just tell them 'I AM' sent you…that should be enough."

That's the kind of reassurance you need. And that only comes through prayer and having a personal relationship with Jesus Christ. The closer you get to him, the more like him you become. Deepening your prayer life isn't just about adding 10 more minutes to your prayers. It's about becoming more transparent and real before God. It's about bringing God everything about you and your life, as opposed to presenting your best. Basically, it's about getting honest.

The more honest you get with God, the more you'll get out of prayer. Tell him how you really feel, and what your true weaknesses are. Let him know where you feel insecure. Ask for his help and guidance. It was only when Moses exposed his insecurity about speaking, did God affirm his purpose. Many times, God waits for us to be honest about our limitations before he responds. We'll wait until we stop pretending and start confessing.

Principle Two: Refuse to be Negative

Certain women can become addicted to negativity. They can't go a day, let alone a few hours, without finding something to complain about. It's as if they feed on negativity and if they don't fill themselves with it, they can't function. They nitpick and criticize to the point that people don't want to be around them. If negativity is poisoning your attitude, you need to starve that appetite. Every time you feel the itch to say, do, or think something negative, pause…and think about whether or not you're adding value to the situation.

The big lie is that negativity is not contagious and only affects you. Being negative is highly contagious and easily spread to those around you, such as your family. A negative mom will raise negative children. Even if they're all cute and innocent now, they are watching how you behave and think. When they become adults, they will inherent your same mindset.

Negativity is conquered one thought at a time, by asking God to shape your attitude. There are no quick fixes. The apostle Paul said, *"Finally, brethren, whatever things are true, whatever things are noble, whatever things are just, whatever things are pure, whatever things are lovely, whatever things are of good report, if there is any virtue and if there is anything praiseworthy—meditate on these things."* (Philippians 4:8).

Close the flow of negativity in your life. If a friend or co-worker's negative attitude affects you, limit your time with them. A negative attitude can sabotage your peace of mind and even causing physical problems. If you're struggling to find joy and contentment, maybe it's because you're looking through the lenses of negativity. No matter what you look at, you always see something wrong.

Make a decision today to reject negative thoughts. As stated earlier, Sarah wasted the good things in her life by focusing on the bad things. But once you refuse to be a negative woman, you can begin enjoying the blessings in your life. You start seeing how the good outweighs the bad, and how different your life would be without Jesus Christ. Learn to celebrate your life and who God created you to be.

Principle Three: Avoid Unhealthy Comparisons

Once Sarah stopped comparing herself with Hagar, God began to open her womb. To compare, is to depreciate what you have and who you are as a woman. It is to devalue your own significance. If you compare yourself to others for too long, you can become disoriented and lose sight of your own purpose.

The root of unhealthy comparisons is a lack of self-confidence. It's seeing something in someone else that you don't see in yourself. This was a problem for King Saul as he compared himself with a younger David.

Coming home from a battle, the women of Jerusalem paraded the streets and sang *"Saul has slain his thousands, and David his ten thousands"* (Ref. 1 Samuel 18:6-9). The bible never mentioned that Saul had a problem killing the enemy. In fact, Saul had an impressive resumé. His military achievements far outnumbered David's at this point. This wasn't about the numbers, but the credit. Saul was bothered that David was getting more recognition.

Saul succumbed to unhealthy comparisons and envy because he lost sight of his own significance. He forgot that the prophet had once anointed him too. So he became egotistic and arrogant. Remember this, arrogance is man's attempt to become significant without God. It is to barter the intrinsic value you already have with counterfeit importance. Arrogance is also a sign of insecurity. When you are secure in your own identity, you don't have to remind others of how important you are. And you certainly don't need the praise of people to feel confident about yourself.

The only healthy comparison you should make is with Jesus Christ. If you want to resemble anyone, resemble the Master. Paul said, *"Imitate me, just as I also imitate Christ."* (1 Cor. 11:1). Furthermore, you were created in the image and likeness of God. It's time to imagine yourself as God has made you: a one-of-a-kind woman with a blend of gifts and characteristics that no one else can replace.

Some other woman will always seem prettier, smarter and better off. Don't spend another minute of your life comparing yourself to what someone else has. You have what YOU have. God designed you the way He saw fit. If he wanted another "Hagar", than he would have duplicated her. But he made Sarah...to be Sarah. The same is true for you. Stop looking at your shortcomings and imperfections as signs that something is wrong with you. Instead, thank God for them! Because every inadequacy, weakness, limitation and imperfection is an opportunity for God to reveal his supremacy in your life.

Principle Four: Keep a Sense of Humor

If you know a little about the life of Sarah, you know that she laughed when God said she would birth a child in her old age (Ref. Gen. 18:11-15). In this case, her laugh was more out of disbelief, rather than joy. As you can see, her faith was still a work in progress.

Later on, when she finally births a son, Sarah named him Isaac, which means "laughter". She said, "God has made me laugh, and all who hear will laugh with me" (21:6). Maybe you're thinking..."Wait a minute; is this the same Sarah from before?"

Something changed in her, and it wasn't just because of the child. Her attitude changed. She realized that no matter what, God is still God—and that everything I go through is merely preparation for what's ahead. She realized that life was too precious, too short to spend on worrying and complaining. Here's the key for you today, don't wait for your "Isaac" to come before you laugh.

138

I know this seems a bit ridiculous, but when did you last chuckle at yourself? The problem so many women have is that they take themselves too seriously. Give yourself permission to laugh at yourself and stop trying to be perfect.

Don't let your flaws or even your failures get to you. Laugh away your worries.

Taking yourself too seriously causes stress. And it's a medical fact that stress is the cause of so many other problems in the body. Some of the effects of stress are fatigue, various aches and pains, headaches, insomnia and even emotional problems such as anxiety and depression. Laughter is one way of avoiding stress. It releases tension and worry. It's one of God's best and most underestimated gifts.

Laughing at yourself will actually boost your confidence, because instead of worrying about your weaknesses, you can focus on your strengths. It keeps your troubles from being blown out of proportion.

Laughter allows you to see that things aren't as bad as you think. It renews your energy and calms your nerves.

Principle Five: Don't let others Define You

Finally, it's time to start seeing your uniqueness as an asset, not a liability. Sarah had to stop worrying about what other people thought of her. She had to be comfortable with herself.

Celebrate the fact that you are who you are. Yes, you're different from the rest! You are not a carbon copy of some magazine cut out or some plastic version of womanhood. Throw away what you think is the ideal Christian woman. Stop putting imperfect women on a pedestal. Sometimes we create our own cookie-cutter idea of what a godly woman is supposed to look like and act like. We put halos on flawed people.

Don't let some picture-perfect ideal define who you are.

Is there room in your life for improvement and growth? The answer is "yes". However, that shouldn't involve changing the fiber of who God created you to be.

More dangerous then letting an ideal define you, is letting your peers define you. Have the courage to be who you are, even if your friends pressure you to be someone you're not. Stay true to yourself, even if you feel the temptation to "fit in". Oftentimes "fitting in" means losing out on your uniqueness.

When a woman strives to fit in, she often falls into the trap of being a people pleaser. The insecurities in her heart create a vast need for approval and acceptance. When she pleases others, she feels better about herself.

When you need compliments or approval to feel good about yourself, you create an unhealthy well of worth. As long as people are pleased with you, your well is full of water. Every positive comment, accepting gesture or action pours a bucket of water in the well.

However, when people are upset with you, reject you, or show unhappiness about you, they draw a bucket of water out of your worth. Sooner or later, your well begins to dry and you find yourself thirsty for acceptance.

This is a terrible way to live. Yet so many women dig this unhealthy well of worth. This is how others can easily manipulate you and use you. And the truth is, they aren't doing anything that you yourself haven't empowered them to do. Letting others define your worth gives them a warrant to take advantage of you. Certain women with ill motives will exploit your "need to please" and move you like a pawn on a chessboard.

I'm not saying these peers are evil, because they themselves have an unhealthy need to be accepted. They themselves have issues of control and feelings of powerlessness. My point is, however, that when you haven't discovered your worth in Jesus Christ, you ultimately give others a pass to push you in every direction. You spend more time caring and listening to what others think about you, than what God thinks about you.

It's important for you to see how easy it is to become a hostage of other people's opinions, instead of God's. Romans 12:2 says, *"And do not be conformed to this world, but be transformed by the renewing of your mind, that you may prove what is that good and acceptable and perfect will of God."* Don't allow yourself to be controlled and influenced by this world (friends, family, co-workers, neighbors, and others you come in contact with), but let God define your worth.

Being a people pleaser empowers others to define your worth. Being a God pleaser allows God to define your worth. Dig a well through your relationship with God—a fountain that never runs dry.

Chapter 12

Trail of Breadcrumbs

Would you leave everything behind to follow God's will for your life? One woman did. Of all the women of the bible I've studied, preached about and used in my books, Ruth tends to be the frontrunner. Her life is a saga of tragedy and triumph, pain and purpose. From losing her husband, to leaving all that she knew in Moab, to following an unbeaten path towards Bethlehem, this Moabite girl had seen her share of struggles. Life had pushed her into a hole of distress — one that many who fall into never come out of.

Bethlehem means "house of bread". So, as Ruth made her journey towards a new life in Bethlehem, she followed the breadcrumbs of Naomi's guidance. However, before I unearth Ruth's personal life, allow me to first pay homage to the flawless picture of redemption painted in her story.

Ruth is a breathing depiction of every sinner—including you and me. A series of tragic events reduced her to the status of an outcast, an exile with slim to zero chance of survival. Hoping against hope, she reached for the grace of her mother-in-law's closest kinsmen, Boaz. The compassion of this kinsmen redeemer purchased Ruth's life and saved her from her inevitable woes.

If you peal back the thick layer of history on this story, you will see how we, like Ruth, were exiled without hope. Our inborn sin reduced us to spiritual poverty. Yet by the sheer grace of our Kinsmen Redeemer, Jesus Christ, we have been purchased, atoned for, and grafted into God's eternal family. Praise God for his grace and mercy upon us all!

The book of Ruth begins with a brief look at the family of Elimelech, his wife Naomi, and two sons named Mahlon and Chilion. A great famine in their hometown of Bethlehem forced them to seek refuge in the neighboring land of Moab—which wasn't exactly the land of milk and honey.

Moab was a rather desolate place, one that didn't have much to offer a hungry family. This gives us a clue into the severity of the famine in Israel, that families considered Moab a viable option. When you're scraping the bottom of the barrel, nearly anything is a grade above. Moab was anything but lavish, but at least it had the smell of something better.

Although Moab was slightly more fertile at the time, the condition of the region proved to be just as harsh. What's worse, Moab wasn't exactly the ideal place for a devout Jew. The Moabite culture practiced the worst of kind of idolatry, paganism and vulgarity. It reeked with wickedness. And last but not least, there was a known history of bad blood between Israel and Moab. They were neighbors, but not very friendly.

Few things are more frustrating than when you escape one awful situation, only to find yourself entangled in a worse one. For Elimelech, the pursuit of a better life in Moab turned out to be nothing more than a dead-end. The dream quickly became a nightmare. And unfortunately, that's where Ruth enters the scene.

Desperate Times

Then Elimelech, Naomi's husband, died; and she was left, and her two sons. Now they took wives of the women of Moab: the name of the one was Orpah, and the name of the other Ruth. And they dwelt there about ten years. (Ruth 1:3-4)

The odds could not have stacked higher against Ruth. The first time her name is mentioned in the scriptures, she is surrounded by a host of tragedies and misfortunes. Elimelech, which means, "my God is king", died before Ruth married into the family. This is a sad situation because the man who represented God's presence and authority in the family is gone. No sooner did he die, did things go south for this family. The same is true for any situation where God ceases to be king. In God's presence we find refuge and security.

Ruth's mother-in-law Naomi was a distressed widow. Naomi, whose name means, "joy", was anything but joyful about her life. Everything she hoped for seemed to vanish. Nevertheless, Naomi was the last remaining pillar in the family, the one holding everybody up and keeping things from falling apart.

Ruth's poor husband, Mahlon, became a victim of desperate times. In fact, his name means "sickly", implying his physical and possible psychological issues. He didn't have a mild case of the flu, but was unhealthy as a way of life. I imagine his constant need of care and dependence made life rather difficult for Ruth.

Her brother-in-law, Chilion, doesn't seem to add much value to the family either. His name means, "weakening".

Like his brother Mahlon, he was unhealthy.

Even though Mahlon probably had some descent qualities about him, the negatives far out-weighted the positives. His life was quickly deteriorating. In fact, his whole future was unpromising and a sure red flag to any bachelorette.

So, allow me to ask the question.

Why would Ruth, a healthy and vibrant young woman be attracted to a man who was weak and dependant? In today's terms, this would be like marrying someone who has a lot of baggage. By marrying Mahlon, Ruth inherited all of his issues. In today's terms, she would have married a man who couldn't stand on his own two feet, a delicate man with unusual needs—financially, emotionally and spiritually.

We generally skip over this chapter in Ruth's life—fast forward to her legendary vow of faith and starlit romance with Boaz. But unless you understand her past, you won't fully appreciate her future. So prepare yourself to see a side of Ruth that perhaps you've never seen.

The honeymoon was barely over before Ruth's husband took a turn for the worse. Ruth 1:5 says, *"Then both Mahlon and Chilion also died; so the woman survived her two sons and her husband."*

Although the bible doesn't say exactly how Mahlon died, his ongoing sickness was most likely the cause. With times being as desperate as they were, he would've had little security against disease and economic downfall. If you're familiar with Ruth's story, you have a basic idea of how she fell in love with Boaz. I'll be discussing that part later.

What concerns me is…why she chose Mahlon?

Mahlon was a problem waiting to happen. Yet Ruth was attracted to him. What was it about her own self-image that she thought she didn't deserve someone promising, someone better? I'm certainly not judging Mahlon, nor am I belittling him for his condition. Life happens. And maybe he was just a product of his father's lapse of faith. However, that still doesn't explain why Ruth would volunteer to be his wife.

Ruth to the Rescue

The way you view yourself, determines what standards you set in your life. Ruth must have felt completely undeserved, or else she would not have settled for less. She didn't see herself as a first-class woman. She didn't value herself. Surely there were plenty of "fish in the sea", other healthy bachelors who could offer her a great life.

Something about Mahlon reinforced what she felt about her worth. It's safe to say that her standards were low, but still, she saw something in this ill-fated relationship that she needed.

What was Ruth thinking? What did she have to gain? Why marry a man with this kind of baggage? If you're married, you may find this discussion helpful in navigating your own marriage. If you're single, and ever wish to marry, read this section carefully.

Have you ever heard a comment like, "I know he's got some problems, but I can fix him." Or: "He'll change after we get married." I'm sure these statements sound pretty familiar. Maybe you know a woman or two who either made comments like these, or believed them, but just didn't say anything. I don't have enough fingers on my hands to count how many times I've seen women enter a relationship with that mentality. It's astounding. I've tried to figure out why women choose guys who are so unstable.

Ruth's first husband was definitely in bad shape. He assumed the role of a victim, and she, the role of a rescuer. Whether she found Mahlon intriguing or challenging, she definitely saw herself as someone who could fix his problems. She thought that by marrying him, things would change and his situation would get better.

But her hopes quickly snuffed. Once Mahlon died, she again felt purposeless and worthless because she gauged her value by how well she rescued others. Ruth was a rescuer. Without knowing what her upbringing was like, I can only imagine that she often played the role of a caregiver or savior in her household. Maybe Ruth's father was also sickly or unstable. Marrying Mahlon, then, would be like marrying her father.

All I can do is speculate, but would I venture to say that this was her comfort zone, a pattern in her life. Being the rescuer in the relationship wears you down. It saps your strength. You slowly and painfully discover that you're lacking support, affection and true joy. You keep pouring out, but nothing is being poured back into you. You love, but feel unloved. You give, but feel bankrupt. You fix others, but feel broken yourself. While there are some small payoffs to being a rescuer, it can take an unhealthy toll on your heart. When a woman plays the part of a rescuer for too long, she sacrifices her own needs.

As long as you play the part of the rescuer, the odds that you will have an authentic relationship based on love, mutual sharing and fulfillment are slim to none. In addition, you run the risk of becoming a victim yourself. As a rescuer, you can easily be taken advantage of and emotionally abused.

As long as Ruth was rescuing, mending or caretaking, she felt valued. She found worth by rescuing troubled people. As long as someone needed fixing, she felt valuable and important. What happens when everyone around you is fine? Then what? Your self-worth begins to crumble. If your worth is connected to rescuing people, when those people leave, so does your worth.

Nobody knows this better than Ruth. Once Mahlon died, the air supply to her soul and significance were cut off.

With no one to nurse, look after, or rescue, Ruth was faced with the challenge of finally taking care of herself. She had to think about what was best for her, possibly for the first time in her life.

I don't know if she held on to any of Mahlon's clothes, perhaps to catch a sniff of him whenever she felt lonely. I can't know for sure if Ruth became depressed or angry. What we do know is that when her mother-in-law Naomi left, Ruth was right behind her (Ref. Ruth 1:6-7).

Ruth was willing to leave it all behind, even though her future was still uncertain. No promises, no guarantees, no evidence that she wouldn't fall back into the same hole again.

Orpah, Ruth's sister-in-law, is a fitting example of a woman who had the same opportunity to leave it all behind, but didn't. Before I discuss Ruth's decision to move on, in the next chapter we will observe Orpah's decision to stay behind.

Chapter 13

Comfortably Uncomfortable

But Naomi said, "Turn back, my daughters; why will you go with me? Are there still sons in my womb, that they may be your husbands? (Ruth 1:11)

Then they lifted up their voices and wept again; and Orpah kissed her mother-in-law, but Ruth clung to her. (Ruth 1:14)

As dysfunctional as Moab was for Orpah, it was still familiar territory. However, this kind of familiarity will limit God's ability to bless your life. Orpah had incentives to stay in Moab. She could continue being the woman she was, and never feel guilty about it. She could play the role of a victim and feel sorry for herself. She could continue to blame others for her problems and complain about issues that she chose not to change.

To think that Orpah didn't have a payoff for staying in Moab is simply untrue. Even though she packed her bags and started the journey towards Bethlehem, she never really left Moab. Something in her wasn't quite ready to cut ties with her former life. She still had an itch to live out her old ambitions.

Sure, leaving Moab sounded nice at the time, but she wasn't completely sold on the idea of changing who she was. She left with reservations.

Orpah felt obligated to go. Maybe she felt like she owed her mother-in-law. Perhaps she didn't want to look like the ungrateful daughter-in-law, who just abandoned her relationships as soon as her husband died. By all accounts, this was a courtesy, not a sincere conviction.

Dealing with Dysfunctions

The real, ugly truth was, Orpah would have much rather stayed in Moab. She wasn't ready to give up her lifestyle, habits and traditions. She wasn't eager to say good-bye the place that she called home—even though home was a mess. Orpah chose Moab over Bethlehem because of a mindset I call "comfortably uncomfortable".

From the outside in, one would assume that Orpah wanted a legitimate opportunity to turn her life around. One would imagine that at the first sight of deliverance, she would seize it.

One couldn't be more wrong.

When you live with a particular problem for any substantial amount of time, you learn to adapt. Your first instinct is to rid yourself of the issue. But when dysfunction is all you know, it actually feels like a safe place. What I'm about to say may sound like a contradiction, but some women cannot function unless there's dysfunction—they cannot live without some sort of conflict, controversy or craziness in their lives.

She's so used to seeing the world upside down that seeing it right side up frightens her. She's so used to family fights that she doesn't know how to live in a family that gets along. She's so used to chaos, that peace scares her. She's so used to nagging to get what she wants, that she doesn't know how to treat a decent husband. She's so used to blaming others, that she doesn't take responsibility for her own actions.

Do you know a woman like this?

Or, are you honest enough to admit that this is you to some degree? Even if it's only a small area of your life, are you comfortably uncomfortable—comfortably afraid, comfortably upset, comfortably bitter, comfortably guilty? If the shoe fits, put it on.

Moab is a cursed place—a place that no matter how hard you try, things always seem to die in your arms. It's a place for women who aren't ready to change, women who are happily unhappy. In Moab, you can be the same woman you've always been. Women don't stay in Moab unless they're gaining something from it. When Orpah turned back, she intended to receive some emotional payoffs.

We all have to confess a certain amount of gratification comes with sympathy and empathy. It feels good, and rightly so. When your heart is grieving or you're struggling, sympathy helps to sooth your emotional sores and mends your wounds. Sympathy helps you cope with loss, discouragement and disappointments. However, it's unhealthy to use sympathy as a source of self-worth.

When you catch the flu and your spouse starts taking care of you, it feels good. All of the sudden, being sick isn't so bad after all—soup in bed, a cushion behind your back, hot tea. Things get comfy and before you know it, you're beginning to enjoy it a little. Sympathy is one way to feel loved and valued. But it's only temporary. Women who are addicted to sympathy are afraid of rejection, because what they actually want is approval and acceptance.

Is there a problem here? Absolutely! You're not being healed. You're not getting any better. Your constant need for sympathy adds unnecessary strain to your relationships— especially your marriage.

Allow me to put it this way: your need for sympathy puts unfair demands on those around you. It creates a high-maintenance living environment in your home and family. It promotes a tense working environment at your place of employment and even your church.

Again, if the shoe fits, put it on. If not, educate yourself on the symptoms so that you don't allow people to take advantage of you.

It's time to experience true significance in Jesus Christ. Nobody understands you more then Him. God created you. He knows how you tick, how you function. Surrender your heart to him today and allow the Holy Spirit to work in your life.

No More Excuses

Victims often possess a license to misbehave while avoiding personal responsibility. They have a mentality that says, "because of what's happened to me, I'm excused to make poor decisions, ignore what I know is right, and treat people how I want". As long as you are playing the role of a victim, you'll never grow and fulfill your true purpose in life. In fact, you will become more critical.

If you're married, your husband is likely to be hurt by your unhealthy behavior. Perhaps you constantly nitpick him and criticize things about him that you used to shrug off. As long as you're the injured spouse, he can't honestly confront the things about you that need to change.

Orpah chose to go back, because Moab didn't require change. She represents women who have the opportunity to move forward, but don't. Orpah was afraid to move on. The thought of embracing a new environment, new rules and new ideas scared her. It's so much easier to return to the place you know—even when that place is unhealthy.

Familiarity is often the enemy of victory. It's a tool that Satan uses to keep you from experiencing what God has for you. Orpah started off on the right track, like many women do, but somewhere along the road she looked over her shoulder. I tend to believe that her reluctance grew with each step, and eventually became apparent to Naomi. Maybe this is why Naomi insisted that Orpah and Ruth go back.

At first, Naomi was fine with her daughter-in-laws following her. Why the sudden change of heart?

It's possible that Naomi began to notice a change in Orpah's attitude and demeanor. At some point, Orpah probably looked pale, unhappy and stressed. This would have provoked Naomi to push them away, for their own good. Orpah felt obligated. Her transition wasn't genuine. No one can ever force you to change. The only one who has the power to make that decision is you. Only you can say, "No more excuses, I'm moving forward".

Chapter 14

Rethink your Relationships

But Ruth said: "Entreat me not to leave you, Or to turn back from following after you; For wherever you go, I will go; And wherever you lodge, I will lodge; Your people shall be my people, And your God, my God. Where you die, I will die, And there will I be buried. The LORD do so to me, and more also, If anything but death parts you and me." (Ruth 1:16-17)

Ruth's attitude was much different than Orpah's. Her vow to Naomi is evidence of a life that has made a complete turnaround. She wasn't looking over her shoulder. Ruth had no regrets, no desire to return to where she's been. Her heart was ready to move on.

Sandwiched between Ruth's famous words are two essential relationships you need in order to live beyond the past.

I believe all that she vowed hinged on these two changes in her life. Let's discuss these two relationships:

1. Relationships with People
"Your people shall be my people"

If you associate with people who represent your old self, you haven't made a complete turnaround. I am not suggesting that you shun or excommunicate your unsaved friends, and become "holier than thou". I'm referring to the people who bring out the worst in you. I'm talking about the people, that after a couple hours of being together, you start talking, acting or thinking like you used to.

If hanging around a certain woman or man tends to bring out your negative side, limit or eliminate your time with that person. You're not condemning them, but that person represents a time in your life that you don't want to relive. It isn't that you don't love them, appreciate certain qualities about them, it's that you aren't the same woman.

That old friend might get bothered with you and say something like "You've changed. I don't know who you are anymore." And if they did, you ought to thank God. Ending a friendship or relationship is never easy. But sometimes it can be a blessing, and completely necessary.

Love them. Pray for them. But move on.

If a certain woman friend brings out an urge in you to gossip about others, lose that friend. If she brings out an impulse in you to spend money you don't have at the mall and feel horrible the next day, lose that friend. If she tempts you to criticize your husband or his family, lose that friend. If she speaks negative against your church and makes you become cynical about your faith, lose that friend.

If you're single, this might be an old boyfriend who has become your security blanket—which you run to whenever you feel afraid or lonely. Every other year or so you find a way to bump into him, email him, or even call him. Dear single sister, let him go. Let bygones be bygones. It isn't fair to you, or to him. Let him move on also. Stop giving him hope every six months when you need a hug or a helping hand. Shred his number, block his emails, do whatever you have to do to cut that relationship off.

What am I trying to say? Relationships are a sign of who you are and where you are headed. Chances are, those relationships came at a time in your life when you hadn't discovered your true purpose and calling. But now that you've turned around and your values have changed, find yourself some new company.

Surround yourself with people of God, people you can learn from, people who make you feel like you ought to pray more, fast more and read more. Get around folks who have dreams and goals, people who are productive, healed, helpful and spiritual. Seek friendships with people who think of church as a means to grow in your relationship with God, not as a religious institution. Connect with people who think before they speak, pray before they make decisions, and think of others before themselves. Surround yourself with those you wish to become like.

Ruth was committed to changing her friends. It is safe to say that nobody in Bethlehem would remind her of Moab, or bring out her old Moabite ways.

The most life-changing, impacting relationship she formed was with Naomi. Now, I understand Naomi didn't exactly "have it all together". She had developed a bitter attitude about her circumstances and was hardly ready to mentor someone. However, Naomi had a spiritual compass. No matter how upset she might have been about her situation, I tip my hat to Naomi's desire for God—His provision and protection.

Ruth clung to Naomi with everything she had. She wouldn't let her go. Interestingly, Naomi is translated to mean "joy or pleasant". There's something about connecting with godly people that brings joy to your life. The right friend ought to create a pleasant atmosphere, not a tense or hostile one. After talking with the "Naomi" in your life, you should walk away feeling pleasant, not stressed, upset or drained.

The right relationships play a huge role in your life. Simply because Ruth held onto Naomi, she plugged herself into a source of unbreakable strength. Naomi would prove to be the best friend Ruth ever had. She would later introduce Ruth to a whole new community of people who worshipped the one true God.

2. Relationship with God
"And your God, my God"

For Ruth to say, "your God will be my God", was a shocking, yet powerful statement. This would mean a complete denial and turnaround from all that she had been raised to believe. It wasn't like she was just changing churches or denominations, but rather a radical revolution of values. Her entire system of beliefs went out the door with one sentence. She threw away years of pagan worship, false ideologies and backwards thinking...for a God that she hardly knew.

It's likely that Ruth esteemed and worshipped false gods while living in Moab. Otherwise Naomi would not have advised her to follow Orpah's lead and return to their gods (Ref. Ruth 1:15). Moab was known for idolatry and paganism. The most recognized and honored god in Moab was named "Chemosh", which means "destroyer".

Many people believe that worshipping idols involves bowing to a wood-carved image or praying to statues. While this is the case for many religions, those little manmade shrines are hardly the biggest issue. What concerns me the most are the other gods (people, places, things or ideologies) we often substitute for the real God.

I suppose this would be an appropriate time to start listing all of those "idols" that can live in your heart. However, I would rather shoot straight for the biggest one of them all.

Are you ready to learn which idol I'm referring to?

Brace yourself, because the biggest idol that stands in the way of women knowing God is none other than "religion". Ruth had religion, not relationship. She had a system of guidelines and an institution of beliefs, but not a close friendship with God. I'm troubled by how many people, men and women alike, who settle for a cheap substitute, instead of the real thing. God never came to establish a religion on earth, but a relationship with His creation. God wants nothing more, then to have a close relationship with you.

Rethink your relationship with God. Do you serve Him solely based on rules and Sunday-to-Sunday routines? Or, do you know God intimately? Assess where your relationship with God is today. Think about how often you pray, fast, and study His word. Perhaps it's time to turn up the heat and change the way you've been relating to God.

Spice-up your relationship with God. Change that same prayer you've been praying for years. Reinvent yourself and let God see a different side of you. Maybe prayer has become drudgery. Perhaps your spirit is thirsty for fresh romance in your personal moments with God.

Chapter 15

Harvesting your Purpose

Bethlehem wasn't the end, but rather the beginning for Ruth. With Moab way behind her, she still had some vital questions to answer:

Where do I go from here?

Now what?

One overlooked aspect of moving beyond your past is discovering what to do with your future. Simply because Ruth made the tough transition didn't mean her life would just naturally unfold. She had to reprogram her thinking and adjust to her new home. The worse thing she could do, as with you today, is to bring your old mentality into your new reality.

Unfortunately, Ruth didn't know how to be anybody else but who she was. I wonder if at first, the whole "new life" seemed a little fake once she realized that she wasn't quite like everyone else. I wouldn't doubt that initially, she felt like she didn't fit in. Nobody knew her or anything about her past. Even though that was a refreshing thought to Ruth, she still needed to find her place and purpose in this new environment.

Anytime you're healed or restored, there is an adjustment period where you begin to reconnect with who you are as a woman. This is a season of discovering who God has created you to be. In fact, this season is so important that how you handle it will determine your destiny.

After reading the second chapter of Ruth, you'll see that she discovered her purpose in the most unexpected way, by doing what any ordinary woman would do.

Since Naomi couldn't do much, Ruth headed off to work. At dawn each day, Ruth joined groups of needy people to glean the fields for leftover food. In those days, the poor were allowed to comb the fields and gather food that was left behind by the harvesters. These were scraps, flawed vegetation that fell along the way.

Interestingly, Ruth's life was much like those scraps left by the harvesters. Her life has broken and seemingly hopeless. Ruth could identify with the food she gleaned, because she too was flawed. However, just like those hopeless scraps, God still had an extraordinary plan for her life.

Handfuls on Purpose

And let fall also some of the handfuls on purpose for her, and leave them, that she may glean them, and rebuke her not. (Ruth 2:16, KJV)

Boaz took interest in Ruth and ordered his servants to intentionally leave handfuls of food for her. He wanted to ensure that Ruth received an uncommon amount of harvest. So Ruth began to pick up those scraps, unaware that Boaz had her best interest in mind.

What seemed like mere handfuls of wheat, were really handfuls of destiny. If you pay attention to the signs around you, you'll discover some handfuls, proof that God has you where you are on purpose. You'll discover His hand at work in your life. The leftover wheat was only a small fraction of what Boaz had in store.

The same is true for you. God has so much to give you. Like Boaz, not only is He wealthy, but He is looking for an opportunity to bless you. Boaz allowed Ruth to glean his fields. He knew that anything she needed, he could supply. Ruth had no reason to go elsewhere. Her needs were met in a way that she had never experienced before.

Look at what the Bible says: "Then Boaz said to Ruth, 'You will listen, my daughter, will you not? Do not go to glean in another field, nor go from here, but stay close by my young women. Let your eyes be on the field which they reap, and go after them. Have I not commanded the young men not to touch you? And when you are thirsty, go to the vessels and drink from what the young men have drawn.'" (Ruth 2:8, 9)

Boaz answered one crucial issue in Ruth's life—hunger. He was able to order his servants to drop wheat especially for her. This was proof that the economy in Bethlehem had bounced back. The worst part of the famine was over.

Ruth was hungry for more then just wheat, but for true significance. God wants you to know that the famine in your life won't last forever. Plus, what the famine has stolen from your heart, your family, your relationships, and your dreams, the Bread of Life (Jesus Christ) will replenish.

God will refill everything that the famine drained from you. Maybe you've sown some tears and planted some pain in the soil of life. Now it's time to receive your harvest! God wants to bless you in uncommon ways.

That's why God allowed you to be emptied. That's why He allowed you to lose some things along the way. If He hadn't done so, you couldn't receive or appreciate what He has for you today. Ruth picked up handfuls of provision because her hands and heart were empty.

The wheat of God's goodness is coming back to your life.

Doors that were shut are going to be opened. Empty places are going to be filled. If you thought about giving up or throwing in the towel, think again. Recognize His handfuls of purpose; they're all around you, waiting for you to seize. God's fields are teeming with blessings.

He has enough power, resources, and grace to sustain you. His desire is that His fields become your fields, His wealth become your wealth. Whatever belongs to Him belongs to you. As Boaz left handfuls for Ruth, hoping to capture her heart, God is leaving handfuls of provision and purpose, so that you will become His.

It's not a bribe, but an invitation.

Ruth carefully demonstrates that how you start isn't as important as how you finish. No matter how ugly or disappointing your past was, you could still become the woman you were meant to be. You could easily sit around, grieve and complain about everything that went wrong. You could come up with excuses why you can't achieve your goals and fulfill your dreams. However, what long-term benefit is there to making excuses?

Orpah went back to Moab because Moab was still in her, and she couldn't separate from it. She missed her divine moment. But Ruth saw beyond her present condition. She heard the call of destiny.

God is preparing you for a great harvest. People and situations you thought you would never get over are now behind you. You may have thought the end of that relationship was the end of your dreams. You may have thought you would never recover from that job loss or car wreck.

But look at yourself today. You're still here!

God sustained you for this moment. It wasn't by accident or chance. It was destiny. Unlike before, God can entrust you with a fresh anointing, a fresh mission. He tested you to make sure you can handle a new level of blessing. What many people fail to realize is that the greater the blessing, the greater the responsibility. God couldn't bless Ruth in

Moab—her past—a place where dreams die. He wasn't going to pour a new miracle into an old mindset. Rather, the Lord waited until Ruth's mentality changed.

The women who live in Moab, never realize their true purpose. They spend their money, time, energy and emotions chasing after ideals and pseudo success. Hopefully by reading this book, you've come to realize that God has so much more to give you. Take your cue from Ruth and maximize the divine opportunities before you.

Chapter 16

Mothering Spiritual Daughters

One day Naomi her mother-in-law said to her, "My daughter, should I not try to find a home for you, where you will be well provided for? Is not Boaz, with whose servant girls you have been, a kinsman of ours? Tonight he will be winnowing barley on the threshing floor. Wash and perfume yourself, and put on your best clothes. Then go down to the threshing floor, but don't let him know you are there until he has finished eating and drinking. When he lies down, note the place where he is lying. Then go and uncover his feet and lie down. He will tell you what to do." "I will do whatever you say," Ruth answered. (Ruth 3:1-5, NIV)

The book of Ruth is really about making life-changing decisions. Whether it was her decision to follow Naomi to Bethlehem, or her decision to exclusively glean in Boaz's field, Ruth stood at more than one crossroad. In a perfect world, life would only consist of no-brainer decisions. But that simply isn't the case. The hardest part about making a decision is figuring out which one is right. Life is not shaped with a cookie-cutter. It's often unclear and unfair.

Thank God for Naomi.

Sometimes it takes a woman with some wrinkles to iron out an uneven path.

Everything Naomi had gone through in her past had given her a panoramic view of life. She knows what it's like to be young, idealistic and even a little whimsical.

Silver strands flowed through Naomi's hair like sterling threads of wisdom. She had been there and done that. She was beyond trying to impress people and far from interpersonal drama. Naomi had what lacks in almost every young woman—experience.

You can't bid for "experience" on eBay or buy it with a credit card. It is a benefit that comes with time and lessons learned. It comes from falling, dusting yourself off and trying again. It comes from heartbreaks and tears, fighting, losing and winning.

Naomi had become a living compass for Ruth—guiding her way in a new environment filled with religious customs and cultural traditions. Along with helping Ruth discover God, she also helped Ruth discover Ruth.

Ruth showed up to Bethlehem not really knowing who she was. She probably left like an outsider, or like an uninvited guest to a party. Naomi helped Ruth to assimilate. Before I address myself to the "Ruth" who is reading this book, I would first like to address "Naomi".

To start, I'm not going to ask your age. I learned very early to never ask a woman how old she is. However, in order to be a "Naomi", a mentor, you must have three essential sights.

1. *Hindsight* – the ability to examine and learn from the past.
2. *Foresight* – the ability to foresee what's coming—both dangers and blessings.
3. *Insight* – the ability to use hindsight and foresight in the present—having intuition, discernment, clear perception, good judgment and practical wisdom.

As you'll notice about Naomi, she possessed all three sights, which qualified her to be a mentor, a spiritual mother. If you consider yourself a mentor, or desire to be one, maybe you're wondering, "How do I develop myself as a mentor and share my three sights with younger women?"

Start by following these five recommendations.

1. Build a relationship

The first words that came out of Naomi's mouth were, "My daughter…" It's impossible to mentor someone without a relationship that is built on trust and respect. Before Naomi ever uttered a tip of advice, she became Ruth's friend. Relationship builds the bridge over the gap that age, background and personality creates. When you really know someone, and have her trust, you can safely mentor without the fear of offending her.

Mentoring without a relationship is nothing more than lecturing. And while lecturing may work in a classroom environment, you simply cannot mentor someone that way. They will shut your advice out, no matter how insightful you are.

Why, you ask?

It all goes back to a phrase I once heard that literally changed my approach to counseling. "People don't care how much you know, until they know how much you care". Thus, relationship provides a foundation where she knows that you care about her. Naomi called Ruth her daughter, when biologically she wasn't. They were not blood relatives. However, there relationship was like the bond between a mother and daughter. I'm not suggesting that you refer to her as your daughter, but rather that you build a trustworthy bond.

Key Point: Mentoring is simply teaching wrapped in relationship.

2. Ask before you tell

Naomi asked Ruth, "Should I not try to find a home for you, where you will be well provided for? Is not Boaz, with whose servant girls you have been, a kinsman of ours?" Before Naomi offered one bit of advice, she asked two questions. Granted these questions were rhetorical in nature, they still provided a doorway into Ruth's mind. One reason asking questions is a smart way to mentor is because it opens up dialogue. It sends a message that says, "I'm listening".

Another reason for this technique is that it forces the other to think for herself. The greatest mentor of all-time was Jesus Christ. The Lord often asked his disciples' questions, hoping they would think hard and search their own hearts. Once he asked his disciples, "Who do men say that I am?" When they answered, "John the Baptist; but some say, Elijah, and others, one of the prophets", he followed up with another question, "But who to you say that I am?" (Ref. Mark 8:27-33)

Jesus didn't ask these questions because he didn't know the answers himself—he asked because he wanted the disciples to examine their own purpose and make a decision about their faith. When mentoring a younger woman, ask her questions that will provoke thought and allow her to make her own discovery.

Key Point: Mentoring is listening before speaking.

3. Shed light, not lighting

As I mentioned, Naomi's questions were rhetorical, hoping to shape Ruth's perspective. Certain women can become easily standoffish when you offer your opinion. The last thing anyone wants is to feel ignorant. There is a fine line between shedding light and lighting. Shedding light is gently opening the blinds in a dark room—giving insight to an area of life that seems murky. Lighting, on the other hand, is more like flipping on the switch and banging a spoon on a pot—a wake up call.

There will be times when you need to flip the switch in someone's life because you sense danger ahead and time is running out. But notice that Ruth wasn't facing any imminent danger. Naomi simply helped her "see" an opportunity that could have a profound impact on her life.

Whoever God has entrusted you to mentor, help her see the obvious without making her feel ignorant or stupid. Remember, you have hindsight and foresight. It took you years to realize and discover what you know today. Put yourself in her shoes. Your wand may not do magic, but it can certainly open the shades of understanding.

Shedding light requires patience. Sometimes, she may not totally grasp your counsel. She might even do the exact opposite. Don't write her off just yet! If you really believe in her, give her some time. Sooner or later she will "see the light".

Key Point: Mentoring is illuminating truth with care.

4. Help her recognize her potential

Naomi instructed Ruth, "Wash and perfume yourself, and put on your best clothes." Essentially, Naomi helped Ruth to recognize her own potential. Spotting potential in someone is only half the battle. A mentor must get her to see and cultivate her own potential. In other words, it's not enough for you to see her potential—she has to know it for herself. Only then can she become confident about her decisions.

Naomi wasn't the Hebrew fashion police. Nor was she interested in opening a beauty salon or boutique. Her advice to soak in a bubble bath, daub herself with Judah's version of Calvin Klein's "Escape", and slip into her best clothes, was an attempt to change Ruth's perception about herself.

Showing up to Boaz's threshing floor in the black of night wouldn't be the best place to model her new look. Therefore, this change of appearance wasn't about attracting a man, as much as it was about setting a new standard. Ruth's makeover was about polishing off the tarnish of past experiences and upsets—scrubbing out the tearstains on her heart and looking like a woman who isn't consumed with regrets. Naomi wanted Ruth to remember how valuable she was. Because the more value you place on yourself, the less likely you are to settle for less.

As a mentor, you have to constantly hold a mirror up in front of her and remind her of who she really is.

Key Point: Mentoring is reinforcing someone's identity.

5. Focus on possibilities

Naomi told Ruth, "Tonight he will be winnowing barley on the threshing floor." By mentioning the word "tonight", Naomi focused on Ruth's present opportunity. Mentoring certainly involves talk about the future. However, don't miss today's potential.

It's possible that Ruth already knew where Boaz would be that night. But she didn't see it as an opportunity to change her life. The spirit of mentoring is helping someone seize the moment and change her life for the good. A mentor's role is to help someone look at realistic possibilities. This is where you need to coach and motivate. As Naomi pitched the idea to Ruth, I can just see her self-confidence rising.

Naomi helped Ruth navigate her options. She said, "go down to the threshing floor, but don't let him know you are there until he has finished eating and drinking. When he lies down, note the place where he is lying. Then go and uncover his feet and lie down." Naomi gave Ruth insight into a custom that she was unfamiliar with. This is where Naomi's hindsight, foresight, and insight really began to pay off. She gave Ruth a beaten path to walk on—some reassurance in a risky situation.

Maybe you don't feel you possess great knowledge or deep wisdom. Maybe you think you don't have much to offer. Nothing could be further from the truth! Your presence alone provides essential support and hope for a woman adrift in uncertainties.

Key Point: Mentoring is not about being profound or philosophical, it's about being transparent and letting your practical wisdom shine.

It's impossible to talk about Ruth, and not mention Naomi. Without her, Ruth would have drifted in a sea of insignificance. She would have never realized her dreams.

You're Covered

It's one thing for a mentor to offer help, and quite another thing for someone to listen. Advice is only as good as it's applied. Once Ruth heard Naomi's advice, she answered with "I will do whatever you say." When God gives you direction, He wants to know if you will follow.

What happened next was literally unimaginable for Ruth. After being widowed and displaced from all that she once knew, God prepared a blessed, loving, and capable man to marry her. As you know, Ruth had to undergo some treatment to deal with her past. Even though Boaz would eventually be her new husband, she couldn't simply jump into that relationship the moment she arrived in Bethlehem.

Ruth had baggage…in all shapes and sizes.

And before embracing a new dream with Boaz, she unpacked the luggage of loneliness, loss and a lousy self-image. Still, however, it all came down to whether or not Ruth was willing to take a step of faith. As the story goes, she not only stepped, but she leaped into her God-given destiny.

Despite hardship and countless challenges, she didn't spoil her hopes with resentment and anger. She could have easily buried her heart in self-pity and shrugged off the opportunity to better her life.

Life isn't fair.

Clouds often block the sunset.

But if you can find yourself in God's grace and discover his endless love for you, surely a ray of sunlight will warm your soul.

God has not forgotten about you. He's placed a "Naomi" in your life. Maybe you just haven't paid much attention. Perhaps you've been focusing too much on your problems that you haven't noticed God's gifts of guidance. Not everyone can be your mentor, your spiritual mother. But certainly someone has influence in your life, a woman whose presence alone brings comfort to your heart.

Find that woman of faith who can be a pillar in your life. Maybe it's your own mother, grandmother, or even a faithful sister in your church. She doesn't have to be family. Sometimes it's better to find someone who isn't related to you. That way their advice is always unbiased and you know your connection is based on something other than your blood. As wonderful as you are, you're mistaken if you think you can make it alone.

Humble yourself. Admit that you don't know it all.

Be teachable and moldable. Because God's heavenly hands are often felt in the human hands of a friend. Boaz, who represents your redemption, is near. In fact, the name Boaz means "strength". All the strength that you lost along the way is coming back to you. Only this time, it's God's unbreakable strength, which cannot be taken away. As Ruth hiked up to the threshing floor and laid down at Boaz's feet, he carefully covered her with the corner of this bedspread (Ref. Ruth 3:8-9).

Coming under the corner Boaz's bedspread suggests something much deeper than keeping warm in a chilly night. It represents Ruth coming under his wing. By this, Ruth actually proposed to Boaz.

Her request was not an indecent proposal, as it might seem. In fact, it was based on two customs in the Mosaic laws: first, the marriage of a widow to her brother-in-law to birth a son, who then takes on the name of a deceased brother; second, the purchase of a family's property by a kinsman-redeemer.

Ruth's life took a dramatic turn. Soon after she married Boaz, she gave birth to a son and named him "Obed". However, what if Ruth had rejected Naomi's advice? What if she had been offended and felt like no one should tell her how to live? What if she was closed-minded? The answer is that she would have never realized the blessings of God. She would have forfeited her true destiny.

Psalm 91:4 says, *"He shall cover you with His feathers, And under His wings you shall take refuge; His truth shall be your shield and buckler."* God wants to cover you—your past, your concerns, and your fears.

Like Boaz covered Ruth under the wing of his protection, God wants you to be his covered girl, his protected, cherished, and beloved bride. Come under Him today. Seek refuge through an intimate relationship with Jesus Christ.

Chapter 17

Beauty and the Beasts

If a complete stranger invited you somewhere, would you go? Let me answer that question for you, "probably not". Going anywhere with someone you hardly know, especially a stranger, isn't a smart idea. Usually you have to really know and trust someone in order to take a ride in his or her car. Following strangers is something that every good parent warns their children about. The thought of your child walking off with a stranger is enough to make your heart race. Apart of any tragic accident, kidnapping is a parent's worse nightmare.

In light of the fact that you should avoid going anywhere with a stranger, I'd like to tell you about one woman who did just that. Now before you raise your eyebrows, I have to inform you that this wasn't just any stranger. What's more, this wasn't just any woman.

I'm referring to none other then Rebekah.

Although Rebekah is a well-regarded woman of the Bible, for her role as Isaac's wife and Jacob's mother, her life hasn't been shared enough. In fact, if you read between the lines of her story, you'll find a pool of refreshing lessons for life. Any woman who wants to answer God's call will pay close attention to how Rebekah responded to hers.

Without spoiling the story, I'll say that Rebekah provides a suitable example of how to step into your God-given calling. However, buckle up. In step with the other women in this book, Rebekah had her fair share of spills and moments she'd like to forget. She didn't always shine.

Unfortunately for her, history cannot be rewritten. Fortunately for you, yours is still a script in progress.

The Matchmaker

In the small town of Nahor, getting a gallon of water wasn't as easy as hopping into your SUV and driving to the grocery store. The simplest chores were strenuous and physically demanding. Both men and women worked long, tedious hours just to put food on the table. As the men labored in the fields, the women shouldered the bulk of the household duties, including raising the children. It was customary for women to restock the basic necessities, especially water for cooking and cleaning.

Sorry, no Alhambra service or Dasani water bottles. Wells were the only place to get water.

Wells were typically located on the outskirts of the village, close enough to walk to, but far enough to build up a sweat under the hostile Mesopotamian climate. So, the women would draw water at the two coolest hours of the day—sunup and sundown. Lower temperatures, however, didn't make the daily treks any less arduous. Women still had to lug heavy jars of water back into their villages. This particular task usually required several roundtrips. Without modern-day conveniences, the rough terrain and back splitting labor aged women much quicker than today.

Welcome to Rebekah's world.

Her day slowly halted just like any other day. The sand chilled and the sun rested its chin on the horizon. After this last painstaking trip to the well and some hot supper, she could finally unwind. Her hair was slick against her forehead as she took a deep breath and wiped the perspiration off her brow.

By now the sun was almost gone and the skies were painted with lavender hues. As always, the other girls were a few steps behind, giggling about something.

Then a subtle sigh of relief came over her as it did every day. For a moment she let the evening breeze carry away her thoughts like dry leaves. Aside from being a few steps ahead of the group, Rebekah towered her peers. Her beauty was arresting. Her eyes sparkled like buffed diamonds and her skin was uncommonly fair. Yet it wasn't just her outward appearance. Rebekah radiated with inner loveliness and humility. She glowed with innocence and virtue.

Walking quickly towards the well she suddenly staggered as she noticed a caravan of men and camels. One man in particular seemed to lock eyes on her. His clothes were faded and tattered as though the sun itself had robbed him. He looked as though he had traveled many miles.

This weary traveler was none other than Abraham's chief servant—whom many theologians believe to be Eliezer. This man wasn't just touring the land for the fun of it. Abraham sent him to his kinsmen to find a suitable bride for his son Isaac. When Eliezer arrived at the well, he prayed for a sign that would reveal Isaac's bride-to-be.

This is what he prayed...

"Behold, here I stand by the well of water, and the daughters of the men of the city are coming out to draw water. Now let it be that the young woman to whom I say, 'Please let down your pitcher that I may drink,' and she says, 'Drink, and I will also give your camels a drink'—let her be the one You have appointed for Your servant Isaac. And by this I will know that You have shown kindness to my master." (Genesis 24:13-14)

Before Eliezer could finish his last sentence, Rebekah approached the well. As his eyes lit up and his heart leaped, he ran towards her. Before we squeeze the juicy details of this encounter, allow me to offer his note of encouragement. The name "Eliezer" means "help". Little did Rebekah know that God sent her some help. Rebekah wasn't in a pinch, or suffering any ailment to my knowledge. She wasn't injured or displaced. In fact, it would appear that she was happy with her life.

So then, why would God dispatch help to someone who didn't need it? The truth is, this help wasn't about restoration, but about a relationship. As previously noted, Abraham sent Eliezer to find a wife for his son Isaac. Otherwise, these two lonesome hearts would have never met. Eliezer was a matchmaker. His whole mission was to bring Isaac and Rebekah together.

In Bible types and shadows, Isaac represents Christ. And Rebekah represents the church. Abraham represents our Heavenly Father who is God. This shadow doesn't dispel the Oneness of God, but depicts the work of God in our lives.

Just like Abraham, our Heavenly Father prearranged the marriage between Christ and the Church (Ref Eph. 5:25-33). Don't let the word "prearranged" bother you. It actually implies that God planned and prepared for this moment in your life. Unlike the movies, the two of you didn't just bump shoulders in an airport and fall in love. But more like God built the airport and purchased an extra ticket just for you.

See the difference?

In Abraham's day, the groom's father would arrange the marriage of his son, including selecting his bride. It was the custom of the culture. In fact, many cultures from the Middle East still practice arranged marriages today.

It's tempting to expound further on this theological point, however, my focus is this: If Isaac represents Jesus Christ, and Rebekah represents you, Eliezer then represents the Holy Spirit, who is the "helper" (Ref. John 14:26).

It is the Spirit who leads us into a personal relationship with God. Romans 8:26 says, *"Likewise the Spirit also helps in our weaknesses. For we do not know what we should pray for as we ought, but the Spirit Himself makes intercession for us with groanings which cannot be uttered."* When you are baptized with the Holy Spirit, the Spirit draws you unto Himself—even speaking for you.

That tug you feel to pray is the matchmaker, helping you to know God deeper. The pulling in your heart for God's presence is the matchmaker, joining you with the groom of your soul.

It's no coincidence that Eliezer met Rebekah at a refreshing place, a place where thirst was quenched. That's where the Holy Spirit meets you—at a place where your spirit thirsts and your heart aches to be refreshed.

The Spirit meets you at your point of thirst.

Eliezer didn't travel all that way just to introduce a religion. He came to introduce a lover, a man she couldn't see with her naked eye. He came to offer her a relationship—which is the backdrop for this whole chapter.

Nothing is more important than your relationship with Jesus Christ. From your relationship flows all the promises and blessings you can imagine. Everything that belonged to Isaac would eventually belong to Rebekah. What was his would soon be hers. Every blessing that God has belongs to you when you enter that sacred relationship.

The matchmaker is betting his life that you'll fall in love with a man you've yet to see. When speaking of the relationship between the church and Christ, the apostle Peter said, *"...Though now you do not see Him, yet believing, you rejoice with joy inexpressible and full of glory."* (1 Peter 1:8)

Eliezer was entirely at the mercy of Rebekah. He couldn't force her against her will. And neither will Jesus. Simply because your marriage to him was prearranged, doesn't mean you're obligated to love him. All he said was, *"...Please let me drink a little water from your pitcher"* (Genesis 24:17).

From there, it was up to Rebekah to respond.

Discovering the Beauty and the Beasts

So she said, "Drink, my lord." Then she quickly let her pitcher down to her hand, and gave him a drink. And when she had finished giving him a drink, she said, "I will draw water for your camels also, until they have finished drinking." Then she quickly emptied her pitcher into the trough, ran back to the well to draw water, and drew for all his camels. (Genesis 24:18-20)

Beauty and the Beast has become one of the most popular fairy tales, largely due to the Walt Disney animated film in 1991. Based on the classic French fable, it tells the story of Belle (meaning "beauty"), a bright young woman disregarded by her townspeople. When her father gets lost in the forest and is detained by an unwelcoming Beast, a once-handsome prince cursed into a monster because he couldn't love, Belle flees to rescue him. The Beast agrees to release Belle's father in exchange for her. Initially disgusted, Belle quickly discovers the Beast's unseen, gentle character.

The only way the Beast could break the spell was to selflessly love another and receive her love in return. When Belle falls in love with the Beast, he miraculously turns into the prince he always was. Belle had to embrace the Beast before she could see her handsome prince.

While Rebekah's "Beauty and the Beast" experience was much different from the classic fairy tale, she was definitely a "beauty" who embraced a "beast".

Eliezer wasn't just looking for any woman, but a special woman. However, in order to identify who she was, she needed to pass a little test that he created. Basically, this unknown woman would have to go far beyond the call of duty.

Let me explain.

In those days, it was customary to offer water to a stranger, especially a thirsty traveler. The fact that Rebekah offered Eliezer some water wasn't a big surprise. That was expected of her. And as you know, we rarely reward those who do what they're supposed to do anyway.

Sorry Rebekah, no points yet.

However, she didn't stop there. Actually, she did something that was so impressive that Eliezer could hardly believe his eyes—even though it was all part of this little quiz.

Eliezer asked God for a woman who would not only get water for him, but for his whole entourage—including his camels. In case you've never watered a camel, which I presume you haven't, it's very different from refilling a dog's water bowl. An average-sized camel can drink up to 30 gallons of water in just a few minutes! Remember the last time you had to carry one or two gallons of milk from your car to your kitchen? Well, imagine carrying anywhere between 250 to 300 gallons, one at a time. That's about how many Rebek-ah had to carry to water all ten of Eliezer's tired camels.

What was Rebekah thinking?

Any other woman would have balked the idea of water-ing 10 camels for a complete stranger. After all, she had plenty of other chores to do. Her plate was full. Then again, Rebekah wasn't just any other woman.

Here's a hint…neither are you.

Keep in mind that this episode is about a relationship and a destiny that Rebekah could have never imagined in all her wildest dreams. This small test of character positioned her for greatness. One outshining principle we can gather from Rebekah at this point is: Special blessings often begin in strange places.

The greatest blessings in your life will not be birthed in beauty, but in seemingly ugly conditions. Nothing was ap-pealing about hauling heavy buckets of water from a well. No glamour, no glitz, just pure sweat. Perhaps halfway through Rebekah started to wonder, "What did I get myself into? This is messing me up. It's messing up my time, my schedule, my priorities, and my likes." Yet, she did it with a smile, a positive attitude. Even though her back ached with pain from bending over and her hands were blistered, she kept on pouring.

The bible doesn't identify the group of women that came with her, but rest assured, there were certainly others. Traditionally, groups of women would come to the well at the same time. Many of them had the same routine. This little gathering at the well became somewhat of a social event. There was talking, laughing and sharing—which lightened up the mood after a hard day's work.

All of the women slowly huddled around the well, possibly waiting in line to refill their pitchers. Surely others besides Rebekah must have seen Eliezer's caravan. A stranger with ten camels and an entourage is sure to draw some attention. Rebekah wasn't the only one who saw Eliezer, just the only one to take interest.

Not only did she possess uncommon kindness and authentic charm, she was willing to distance herself from the status quo.

Rebekah had to step away from the ordinary, the routines of life in order to entertain a strange man. But remember what the Apostle Peter said, *"Beloved, do not think it strange concerning the fiery trial which is to try you, as though some strange thing happened to you; but rejoice to the extent that you partake of Christ's sufferings, that when His glory is revealed, you may also be glad with exceeding joy"* (1 Peter 4:12-13).

Isn't it ironic that the most beautiful woman in the bunch, volunteered for the ugliest job? What an oxymoron. A beauty embraced a beast. Dear woman, maybe there are some "beasts" in your life that seem unfair and unjust. Maybe you're at a point where you feel burdened by a beast in your home, your job, your finances, your ministry or your relationships.

It's crucial that you make the distinction between the "beasts" and the "barriers" in your life. The difference between a beast and a barrier in life is this: a beast is a burden that God allows you to carry for a divine purpose. A barrier is an obstacle setup by the enemy to derail your purpose. A beast, although painful, will always draw you closer to God. A barrier will always come between you and God.

The one thing that the enemy doesn't want you to know is that the beast will take you to the bridegroom. The same beast that Rebekah tirelessly watered transported her to Isaac. Little did she realize that she actually fueled her own destiny. Once she accepted Eliezer's offer to marry Isaac, she would then saddle up on the very animals she nourished. When she poured water into those pitchers, she poured out the miles needed to reach her destination.

The burden you've been carrying is positioning you for something great. Keep pouring. Keep nourishing yourself. Soon the very thing that has brought you distress will bring you joy. Others may not understand your passion and your willingness to pour into a cause that seems futile. Perhaps they think you're wasting your time and energy on a hunch that you can't prove. Rebekah's peers must have thought she was crazy.

Why go the extra mile?

It's not like Rebekah knew why this stranger had come. At the time, she had no idea what brought him. So we can't assume she worked double to get what she wanted. Amazingly, Rebekah served them out of the goodness of her heart. She wasn't looking for a blessing, but to be a blessing. She wasn't interested in receiving, but giving.

God is searching for a woman like Rebekah, a woman who will lay down her personal agenda. As beautiful as she was, Rebekah wasn't consumed with herself. She was selfless, virtuous and graceful. There is nothing attractive about a beast. However, God uses the foolish to confound the wise. He uses the beasts to reveal his beauty. The question is: are you willing to water some burdens in your life, for the sake of your divine destiny? Are you willing to embrace a beast of burden in order to behold the beauty of God?

Chapter 18

Avoiding Mr. Wrong

While the spiritual angle in Rebekah's story is ripe with insight, I can't afford to overlook the practical lessons, the life tools that make the bible ever so relevant. This particular segment might seem like a detour for married women, but for single women who haven't found "Mr. Right", this is actually an avenue you can't afford to miss. Even if you are married, this chapter may provide some honest feedback about your life, and empower you to make better decisions in the future. If you have a daughter who is unmarried (younger or older), this chapter can also help you point her in the right direction.

Aside from your relationship with God, your next most important relationship is with your spouse. If you're single and ever plan on getting married, Rebekah can teach you some things about avoiding "Mr. Wrong".

You know better than anyone that emotions can sometimes become blindfolds. In your quest to live your dream you may end up ignoring some glaring red flags. In a culture that tends to put more focus on the wedding day then the marriage, it's easy to lose sight of what really matters in life.

Magazines pile up every spring telling you how to become a bride. But few ever tell you how to become a wife. After the cake is cut and the bouquet is tossed, how do you really know that you picked the right man for your life? What will keep your marriage glued together during the tough times? What small quirks will become big issues in two years? Selecting the right mate is one of the most important decisions you'll ever make.

Isaac was by all accounts, "Mr. Right". The right man, based on your values and goals, is out there. But in order to know the right type, you have to know the wrong types. Too many single women waste time and energy on a relationship that was vague from the get-go. I can't tell you how many times I've heard phrases like, "I thought he was the one", or "Everything was good until he changed."

Let me save you some heartache by introducing three "Mr. Wrongs" you should avoid:

1. The Mannequin

With the mannequin, perception is everything. He looks the part, talks the part, wishes the part, acts the part, but sadly doesn't live the part. His crowning attributes are usually his appearance and charm. He's usually a handsome fellow and pays a lot of attention to how he's perceived by others. For him, image is an asset, not a liability. This attitude also fuels jealousy and male bravado. In other words, he's somewhat narcissistic. In the beginning of your relationship with the mannequin, these traits and behaviors seem harmless and kind of cute.

It seems as though he's independent and driven. In fact, he's probably successful in his career and is quickly climbing the corporate ladder. Although he's dated a lot in the past, nothing too serious, he really wants to settle down. But keep in mind; he's mainly after an "ideal". So he's not as interested in how you think, your values, your needs, your goals, but your appearance—how you will look standing next to him at the company banquet or even a church event. All this adds up to the fact that he sees you more as a possession, a prize, and a fixture.

Women who marry mannequins find that the same suave personality that wooed her in the beginning is a bit controlling. Not all charming men are mannequins. I don't want to scare you. But oftentimes the too-good-to-be-true guys usually are. Here are questions you need to ask:

A. What's underneath his looks and charm?

Consider for a moment that Isaac's physical appearance or charisma played no role in Rebekah's decision to marry him. Maybe you're thinking, "Physical attraction is important". However, in today's culture, it's way overrated and puffed up. People today are appearance-driven.

Nowadays, it's all about how you look on the outside. From cosmetic surgery to Botox, people are becoming more and more obsessed with the superficial. You want a husband with depth, someone who can talk about things other then himself. A certain amount of intensity is healthy because it keeps things interesting.

B. Besides making money, what drives him?

Things, not people or purpose usually drives mannequins. He wants to make more, so he can get more. This is where he places the most value. And consequently he will attempt to use this method to buy your affection, and your children's love. He'll think that working long hours to give your children "the best" is better than spending quality time with them. When he is compassionate, it's usually motivated by guilt. You want a husband who is driven with purpose, a man who places more value on people rather then things.

C. How is his relationship with God?

When Rebekah arrived with Eliezer's group, Isaac was meditating in the fields. Her first impression of him was that he was a man of faith, a man who knew God. His allegiance to God was out in the open. Mannequin men have a reputation of being spiritually shallow or stagnant. There's nothing too deep about their relationship with God, because again, it's about perception.

The fact that he's a church-goer doesn't mean he's interested in growing his relationship with God, or that God's kingdom is a priority in his life. His roots are basically surface-level and he sees church as more of an obligation or routine. How do you know? Because he doesn't have much conviction about the principles of the Bible, apostolic truth, or much respect for spiritual authority. His liberal mind about faith and religion may seen appealing at first, but into the marriage you'll need someone with strong convictions, someone who will keep your family grounded.

Don't let a mannequin sweet-talk you. Get to the bottom of who he is and really decide what kind of husband you want. Why didn't his last relationship work? It's easy to get overwhelmed by his charm and lose sight of the things that really matter. If he's going to be the leader in your home, make sure he's got some substance to him.

2. The Mama's Boy

Be prepared, because mama will always come first. For some reason, he was never able to cut the cord, and whether openly or privately, his mom takes priority. He's usually quite nice, polite and particular. His greatest quality is that he treats his mom well (although some mama's boys can take advantage of their mothers). And what attracts you to him is that you figure, "If he treats his mom well, he'll treat me well". This statement is both true and false: true, because how he treats her is important, and yet false, because it can also come between you. But beware; the latter tends to be more common.

A true mama's boy will never admit it, but he's actually afraid to disappoint her. That's why he excuses her behavior and comments, even when they directly or indirectly offend you. Instead of confronting her about her sarcastic comment, he not only pardons her, but he defends her. While she may know her influence, the root issue is not his mother. She only does what he lets her do. She only says what he lets her say. The root issue is that he hasn't grown up.

He's a boy, not a man. And boys need mothers to tell them what to do, to baby them and do everything for them. If you marry him, guess what he's going to expect from you? A man who is a boy inside tends to be needy, angry and confused. He also tends to cling and shy away from conflict. His masculinity is fragile and easily threatened, either because he didn't have a strong male role model, or because his mother constantly sheltered him.

When Rebekah married Isaac, his mother Sarah had already passed away. As special as Sarah was, she wasn't around to dictate Isaac's life or interfere in their marriage. Assuming your future mother-in-law is alive, your husband must distance himself (emotionally, and sometimes geographically) from her in order to fully embrace you. This is what the bible refers to as "leave and cleave". Genesis 2:24 says, *"Therefore a man shall leave his father and mother and be joined to his wife, and they shall become one flesh."*

Isaac was ready for Rebekah because he was free from mama's control. The man you consider to marry must be free from his mother's daily control. If he's over 30 years old, and still living with his mom, proceed with caution. Just make sure he's balanced. Watch how he handles situations regarding his mom. Does he tell her too much about his personal life?

If this bachelor is not willing to leave his mother's nest and cleave to you, re-evaluate before you say, "I do". It may not seem like a big deal now. But down the road you will struggle and compete for priority. The fact that mama always calls during dinner or needs something small at the same time you do, won't be your biggest problem. It's that he'll immediately respond.

Let's look at one more Mr. Wrong.

3. The Mess-Up (a.k.a. Loser)

I know the title for this one sounds harsh, but allow me to explain. He doesn't know what he'll do without you. Sounds romantic, right? Problem is, you hardly know him. You are his ticket, his reason for "wanting to get better or get spiritual". Again, sounds nice, right? Problem is, he isn't motivated to get better without you. It would appear that he's been down on his luck lately. The Internet-based business that he and his buddy started six months ago went belly up. Now he's in the hole ten thousand dollars and the creditors are calling. This venture came after a bad investment in a multi-level marketing business that ended up being a scam.

His desk is stacked with yellow notepads and stickies with plans, ideas, and contacts. He's probably a clever salesman, which is part of the reason you're still talking to him. This guy can sell ice to Eskimos, beachfront property in Arizona—you get the point. Yet with all his wit and impressive goals, he can't seem to nail down one stable job. He struggles with authority figures and can never get along with his bosses. According to him, the company didn't know what they were doing, didn't see his potential, or blacklisted him from day one.

The mess-up has a story to tell about every job he lost. In fact, everyone else is to blame for his situation, but him. If only the right person would believe in him, he would accomplish so much. However, he tends to be a little flakey — always a little late, but with good reason, always a little short on cash, but will pay you back.

He would be an easy guy to ditch if his heart wasn't so big, if he didn't love kids and he wasn't such a good listener. However, he has a lot of suspicious areas to him, and he tends to stretch the truth. Okay, he lies. You've caught him in several lies, but never challenged him because you pity him.

That's where he gets you.

Getting into a relationship with the mess-up is like playing Russian roulette with your emotions. Everything can explode in your face at any moment. Not only will he end up breaking your heart, but he'll break your checkbook. The mess-up typically doesn't have his finances in order, and is usually in serious debt. Besides his charm, he doesn't have much to offer. If you marry him, you will inherit his debt, poor investments and hazy ambitions. His burned bridges will become yours. His reputation will be linked to yours.

Is this what you want?

Isaac didn't need Rebekah to make it. He had something to offer, something to give. He was balanced and reliable. When Rebekah came to him, Isaac had a stable and secure home. He was also a gentleman, and treated Rebekah with respect, honor and dignity.

Maybe you're thinking, "Well, neither of these three men reflect the man I'm interested in." If that's the case, you still need to read the next segment. Now the focus is on you.

Love with Brains

Now that we've uncovered some Mr. Wrongs to avoid, let's shift the spotlight towards you. Assuming you found whom you believe to be Mr. Right, there are still some timeless lessons you can learn from Rebekah. We have all heard the phrase "love is blind" — which implies that when you're in love, you tend to overlook the negative aspects of your partner. You minimize imperfections and downplay certain attributes that you normally wouldn't accept. In some senses, this can be a positive outlook simply because we all have little flaws and physical blemishes.

However, oftentimes "love is blind" goes too far, even overlooking serious character flaws and behavior you would normally oppose. Blind love in many cases is actually "dumb love", meaning you refuse to acknowledge or accept negative characteristics about that person. Because of one or two positive things about this relationship, you'll ignore the red flags.

Love must be smart. As difficult as that may sound, it's the only way to build a happy, healthy marriage. Only listening to your heart will get you into trouble. When it comes to relationships, you need your mind too. Simply because you "love" him, isn't enough. Do his plans line up with your plans? Do his values match your values? Do crucial aspects about his behavior bother you? What kind of family does he come from? How do they treat you? Think ten years down the road. What things do you know about him now that will be a major issue later on? These questions may seem unromantic and unexciting, but if you ignore them now, you'll revisit them later. Only then, it may be too late.

Blind love has it's own motto. Here it is: "I can change him".

That's the biggest mistake you can make. It is downright absurd to believe that you can change a man who has been, believed or behaved a certain way his whole life. Who he is...is who he is. It's all or nothing. Don't let your heart pull the plug on your good judgment. God gave you a sound mind. And with it, you can become a smart lover, who is ultimately a happy lover. Below are some classic tips to loving smart.

1. Wait to be pursued

Instead of letting the man pursue you, the tables are turned, and now you are pursuing a certain man. This role reversal isn't healthy. And while some women may have some success, women who become "desperate" usually settle for less. Rebekah didn't pursue Isaac. In fact, she didn't even know him. However, the servant was drawn to her inner radiance and character. Work on your godly radiance, your inner and outer beauty. Take care of yourself. Smile a lot. Get closer to God. Let your light shine from within. God has prepared someone to pursue you.

Never make the first move. It sends the wrong kind of message. Most secure men are not attracted to such boldness and aggressiveness either. Let him pursue you. And if he doesn't, you know what that means.

2. Listen to family

Before Rebekah left with Eliezer, she first met with her family. Her older brother Laban talked with Eliezer about Isaac and learned as much as he could. She didn't just ride into the sunset without getting her family's blessing. Her brother told Eliezer, *"The thing comes from the LORD; we cannot speak to you either bad or good. Here is Rebekah before you; take her and go, and let her be your master's son's wife, as the LORD has spoken"* (Genesis 24:50).

Maybe you're in a relationship with a man where no one in your family seems to like or connect with him. Don't let the pulse of romance and idealism fog your clarity about real life. Unless your family is completely senseless and unreasonable, their say, blessing, opinion and advice should matter to you. Oftentimes your family and friends have a different vantage point and may see certain things that you don't see, are in denial about or believe will change. Their disapproval probably frustrates you, because in your mind, you see something in him that they don't.

This is typically the biggest mistake women make. They follow their hearts, instead of their minds. If it were a business or investment decision, you would back away immediately. But your heart is overruling your mind, even though certain warning signs are blatantly obvious. Love and romance have a way of masking issues that you would normally avoid. Change your focus. Look from the outside in.

3. Make God the priority

The day that Rebekah met Isaac, he was meditating in the fields. This is significant because it reveals what kind of man he was. His relationship with God was no secret. From the beginning, Rebekah had a clear understanding about his faith and convictions. It was no mystery that God was the number one priority in Isaac's life. This wasn't an attempt to impress her either, but rather clear proof of his relationship with God.

Before giving your heart, your life to someone, determine if you are spiritually compatible. Is God a priority in his life? Does he just attend church, or does he have a true relationship with God? What types of convictions does he have? Is he a praying man? Or is his faith a riddle, a mystery you can't seem to pinpoint? Does he possess a reverence for God and the bible? Answering these questions beforehand will prevent a struggle for spiritual synergy in your home.

Right now, you may be so wrapped up in his charm, good looks or promises, that you aren't paying much attention to his spirituality. Simply because he attends your church or is apart of your denomination doesn't qualify him as a lifelong partner. After the honeymoon you're going to want a husband with a godly spine, who takes stands and isn't constantly questioning his beliefs. Don't let your life be an experiment. His open-mindedness about faith and doctrine may be likable at first, but his constant wavering and lack of certitude will create tension in your marriage—especially when it comes time to teach your children.

4. Stay connected to your friends

As Rebekah headed off to meet her groom-to-be, the bible says that she took her nurse and maids with her (Ref. Gen. 24:59, 61). Although she left her old way of life, she didn't abandon the women who had supported and nurtured her. One of the signs of an unhealthy relationship is when the man pulls you away from your friends. Of course, as the desired woman, it's difficult to see this happening. Your potential husband should not separate you and your friends, but be able to mix with them. Some women are known for this. As soon as she gets a boyfriend, you don't hear from her for two months. Sound like someone you know?

My advice to you is, don't isolate yourself from the very friends who have been there for you, long before prince charming came along. This doesn't mean that you need to spend every waking moment with them, but don't become a stranger all of the sudden. If things don't work out with him, you'll be looking for those same friends you forgot about. The reunion may not be so smooth.

If your love interest can't seem to get along with, connect, or intermingle with your friends now, he won't later. If your friendships mean a great deal to you, this is something you must consider.

5. Don't reveal too much, too soon

Another love pitfall comes when women reveal too much, too soon. You will notice that just before Rebekah met Isaac, she covered herself with a veil. This is believed to be the origin of what Jews call *bedeken* (veiling), where brides would veil themselves during the wedding ceremony. I believe we can gather some modern day application from this practice. Sometimes revealing too much, too soon, isn't good for the health of the relationship. If you disclosed information about your personal past, family secrets, mistakes, issues and dreams, and you just met last week, things are moving way too fast. Preserve yourself—not only sexually, but emotionally.

Here's the main problem with revealing too much, too soon: if things don't work and you go your separate ways, he still knows all of your business, including the "laundry". You have no means of tracking whom he tells, directly or indirectly, about your personal life. Why would you want someone you hardly know carrying around personal information about you or your family?

Take things very slow. Just because he shares everything right up front, don't feel obligated to do the same. In the beginning of any relationship, veil yourself with conversations that focus on "light" matters, current events, daily happenings and/or church activities. Don't give him the final chapter until he's read the introduction and prologue.

This also helps to prevent the relationship from turning sexual. Especially in cases where you've both made lots of bad decisions or have broken pasts. There is a tendency to want to comfort each other, and physical acts such as hugging can easily cross the line into something more sensual.

The purpose of this advice is not to scold you, but to empower you to make decisions that you won't regret. Even if you found Mr. Right, it might be the wrong timing. As I said in previous chapter (in a different context), the right thing, at the wrong time, is the wrong thing. If school is a priority right now, finish it. If you have other financial goals or personal desires you want to fulfill, do it now. If he's the right one, it will happen at the right time.

If you are married, I haven't forgotten about you. As you'll see, Rebekah had some pressures to deal with once she was married. We'll look at those pressures in the next chapter.

Chapter 19

Pressure Points

Isaac and Rebekah's wedding was noting short of a storybook romance. In fact, Rebekah could not have asked for a better way to begin her journey. However, there was one problem that seemed to amplify as those first tender years of marriage began to slip away. Soon it became apparent that Rebekah was infertile.

Not until Rebekah married her dream husband and settled down did she realize that something within her was broken. When she was younger, she had no need to bare children. So whatever was wrong inside wasn't a problem. Something can be wrong, and yet not be a problem. Something that's wrong doesn't become a problem until it's needed.

If your hand is broken, something is definitely wrong. But it's not a problem until you need to write or turn a doorknob. Your heart may be broken, and may even ache from time to time, but it's not a real problem until you try to love someone.

Maybe you're dealing with things right now that five or ten years ago you never imagined would be a problem. Maybe you're struggling with an issue that was dormant for years, but just now has come to the surface. Like Rebekah, you're trying to draw from an area in your life that's been depleted. And maybe you're even wondering how this happened. All of the sudden, a weight is added to your life that you never had to carry.

Rebekah's picture perfect life wasn't so perfect anymore. All eyes were on her, as the Promise nation hinged on her ability to birth a child. The human body is made up of various pressure points—areas that when contacted will produce significant pain. Martial artists are known to target and strike the body's pressure points to maximize the impact and accomplish a certain outcome. For instance, striking one pressure point could achieve more than several blows of brute force.

Every woman has pressure points, areas in life that if contacted can produce significant pain. Rebekah was no different, and neither are you. Although we could compile a master list of all the pressure points, I've categorized them into three areas based on Rebekah's experiences:

1. Feminine Pressures – This pressure represents all the issues that are exclusive to women. Every woman was expected to produce children. Aside from being a good wife, nothing was more important than being a mother. This was likely the single greatest achievement for a married woman. Unfortunately, Rebekah was infertile.

2. Family Pressures – Rebekah joined a family who walked by faith. No only that, her mother-in-law Sarah dealt with and overcame the exact same problem. Sarah's success would have put some pressure on Rebekah to follow the family path.

3. Faith Pressures – Rebekah knew that Isaac's legacy depended on a son. She didn't just marry any man, but the son of Abraham himself. Even within the faith system, there are pressures to measure yourself up against the godly and somehow etch your story.

Can you somehow relate with Rebekah? Something inside of her was dysfunctional, and on top of that, she has all these expectations to meet. It's enough pressure to make anyone buckle. Even though she's broken inside, she can't even grieve properly because so much was riding on her. Maybe you're going through a time right now when the pressure points are being pushed. Demands at work, at home and even at church are stressing you out. You're sucked into a hole where every time it seems like things are getting better, they get worse.

Rebekah's struggles created a perfect storm in her life. First, she's dealing with an issue that she always had, but didn't surface until now. Second, she feels the pressure to produce something she physically cannot do. As strong of a woman as she was, she had to realize that there are some things you cannot do on your own.

Genesis 25:21 says, *"Now Isaac pleaded with the LORD for his wife, because she was barren; and the LORD granted his plea, and Rebekah his wife conceived."* When Rebekah ran out of words and seemed to loose her breath, her faithful husband stepped in. If you recall, I began Rebekah's story by portraying her marriage as a representation of your relationship with Jesus Christ. With that in mind, this is when relationship pays off. When you've run out of answers, run out of solutions, and you don't know what more to say, the Holy Spirit will intercede for you. He will say what your mouth cannot utter, your lips cannot speak, your heart cannot express (Ref. Romans 8:26-27).

In order for the Holy Spirit to intercede on your behalf, you must learn to let go. Isaac was 40-years-old when he married Rebekah. They didn't have children until he was 60-years-old. If you do the math, roughly twenty years went by before Isaac prayed for his wife.

I can only speculate, but consider this observation. Either Isaac lagged twenty years to finally pray for his wife; or it took twenty years for Rebekah to let it go and allow him to pray for her. Judging by how much Isaac loved Rebekah and by the intensity of his plea, I can't imagine he purposefully held out. This was a case where Rebekah internalized her problem, owned it, and maybe even blamed herself for not being able to fulfill her role.

It didn't take Isaac twenty years to finally care and do something about it—rather it took twenty years for Rebekah to let go and realize that she couldn't fix it by herself. My concern is for women who carry internal weights for ten, fifteen, even twenty years until they finally crack and say, "Okay God. I can't hold this any longer. I surrender it to you." Any issue you carry for that long is emotionally and physically unhealthy. After a while, it sucks the strength and joy out of your life like a leech.

Dear woman, sooner or later you have to realize that you've done all you can do, and that holding on to that issue is only hurting you more.

Why have you been holding on, internalizing, blaming, feeling guilty, feeling embarrassed, holding grudges for this long?

What progress have you made?

What good has come from it? Why should you spend the second half of your life suffering from things that happened in the first half of your life? Why should yesterday rob you of today?

I pose these questions because I believe it's time for you to let go. And I don't mean this meager, half-hearted surrender you give occasionally after a touching sermon. I'm talking about complete abandonment, a total and utter desertion where you say, "God, I'm through carrying this. I'm done feeling this way about it. I've reached my limit. I'm tired of shouldering this issue. It's yours. I disown it. Only you can fix what's broken within me. Lord, I quit!"

Quitting isn't such a bad thing when you put it in proper context. Sometimes the best thing to do is quit. When you're fighting a battle that doesn't belong to you, it's time to quit. When you're crying and anxious about cares that God has repeatedly asked for you to give up, it's time to quit.

As much as Isaac wanted to take over, he couldn't. The same is true between God and you. No matter how willing he is to bless and touch your life, he will only go where you grant Him access. After Isaac stepped in and pleaded before the Lord on Rebekah's behalf, the Lord answered.

One earnest prayer did...what twenty years of worrying could not do. Imagine what could happen in your life, if you simply let go of the things you've held onto so long. Imagine the fresh blessings, the renewed strength, and the unshelled joy that waits.

What are you waiting for? Surrender it all today. Right now. This could be your moment for a breakthrough. But you'll never know unless you let go.

Sweet Sorrows

I can't help but wonder what Rebekah was feeling when she said, "If all is well, why am I like this?" This single statement opens the lid on Rebekah's heart and reveals a jarring reality about life—a dilemma we all find ourselves in at one point or another. Rebekah was stuck in the middle of sweet sorrows, an oxymoron of life.

The word oxymoron signifies two separate, but conjoined concepts. It is a combination of opposites, or a union of contradictory ideas. As I see it, there were two sweet sorrows, two areas of life where an oxymoron existed. Perhaps you will relate to one, if not both in your life.

Sweet Sorrow #1: Happy, but Troubled

Rebekah's first sweet sorrow was that she was happy, but troubled at the same time. As previously mentioned, Rebekah was married to Isaac. He was not only the son of Abraham, but also an heir to God's promise. What intrigues me is that his name means "laughter".

I assure you, however, that his name wasn't the punch line to a joke. Laughter is serious business to God. That alone may seem like an oxymoron because most people think of laughter as a momentary reaction to something we see, hear or feel.

Yet in God's eyes, laughter is the outward expression of joy. Nothing has to be funny or comical in order to have joy. Unlike happiness, joy isn't based on circumstances, but rather on the goodness of God. Laughter is also an expression of confidence. Psalm 2:4 says, *"He who sits in the heavens shall laugh; The Lord shall hold them in derision."* God laughs because he is fully confident about his ability to defeat his enemies. He laughs because he's in control. When we place our joy in the Lord, we also have confidence and faith about our circumstances.

I briefly shared some insight about laughter so that you could understand whom Rebekah was married to. She was married, joined together with laughter. The joy and confidence of God was in her home. The reassurance of God's faithfulness was within reach. Isaac had the innate ability to laugh about matters that others would be threatened by. After all, here was a man who stared death in the eyes when his father was ordered to sacrifice him—only to walk away without a scratch.

Yet in spite of this glaring gift in Rebekah's life, she felt despair inside. In the morning, she opened her eyes to laughter. But by nightfall, she wiped tears of frustration.

Have you ever been torn between two emotions? You're thrilled about your new career, but hurting over a lost relationship. You're excited about your ministry, but frustrated with a decision that your son or daughter made. You feel blessed in one area of your life, but cheated in another.

One moment you're thankful.

The next, you're regretful.

Like Rebekah, every woman goes through times when life seems painfully unbalanced. One area of your life feels great, while another area feels uncomfortable. One area of your life makes you laugh, while another area makes you weep. Even though Rebekah was married to laughter and joy, she privately suffered from depression-like symptoms.

Simply because you are joined together with Jesus Christ, the essence of joy and confidence, doesn't exclude you from seasons of despair. The Lord could be in your house, within reach of prayer, but yet you feel overwhelmed with the issues of life.

How can this be possible?

The answer is that just because the Lord is in your life, doesn't mean you have fully let go of your worries and embraced his presence. Consider the story of Mary and Martha where Jesus sat in their house. Only one sister fully immersed herself in his presence, while the other remained worried and troubled about many things.

Rebekah had laughter, joy and confidence sitting in her home, but the worries within consumed her thoughts. All of the sudden the one that understood her pain and loved her more than anyone was blocked out.

I wonder how often you have done this?

How often have you blocked out the Lord because of the many worries that war within?

I believe we're all guilty of this from time to time. Rebekah was no different. But you'll see in a moment that her sweet sorrow became a sweet surrender.

Sweet Sorrow #2: Expecting, but Struggling

But the children struggled together within her; and she said, "If all is well, why am I like this?" So she went to inquire of the LORD. And the LORD said to her: "Two nations are in your womb, Two peoples shall be separated from your body; One people shall be stronger than the other, And the older shall serve the younger" (Genesis 25:22-23).

Rebekah's second sweet sorrow was that she was expecting, but also conflicted inside. After years of waiting, Rebekah finally became pregnant. I imagine that news of her pregnancy created quite a stir of excitement in the camp.

I clearly remember the day we told my parents, and in-laws, that my wife Cherie was pregnant with our son, Makai. We held the secret for about a month and then on Christmas we announced the news. The living room erupted with excitement, as we hugged, laughed and shared a moment of joy. I also remember the first time that the baby began to move. They were soft and cute little nudges. You had to look real close in order to see her tummy move.

However, as weeks became months, those little nudges became little soccer kicks. Sitting across the room I could see Cherie's tummy shift as the baby moved. Then came the karate kicks around full-term! Every now and then my wife would say "ouch" or "uh" when our little guy would suddenly move. Although these movements were uncomfortable, and sometimes painful for Cherie, they were also normal.

First, I want to mention that sometimes the things we fight and worry about are simply normal occurrences in life. Sometimes we beg God to heal or remove something that is normal, a reality of life. Not everything you go through is an attack of the enemy or reason to fight back. Life is comprised of stages and seasons. Ecclesiastes 3:1 says, *"To everything there is a season, a time for every purpose under heaven."* If you read the next seven verses, you'll see all the different seasons we go through.

On the contrary, anytime a significant purpose is at stake, there will be conflict. Rebekah's pregnancy wasn't totally average, because in her womb were twins. To add further complexity, these twins were not a duet, but two opposing concepts. The kicks that my wife used to get with our son are nothing compared to the painful struggle inside of Rebekah's womb.

The bible says that the children struggled within her. They weren't playing, but fighting for position and power, even before they were born! These fraternal twins were Esau and Jacob — two brothers that were nothing alike.

Perhaps you're like Rebekah. On one hand, you're excited about the future and expect great things to happen. On the other hand, there is a painful struggle going on inside of your heart—the birthplace of your dreams. One side of you is comfortable with average and playing it safe. The other side of you seeks adventure and risk. One side of you seems to crave things that are spiritual unhealthy. The other yearns for deeper intimacy with God.

The struggle within is simply an internal conflict. It could be a struggle within your family, your home, your marriage, your career, your ministry, your church, or just within your own heart and will. Only you and God know where the inner struggle is.

Why is there such a struggle?

When God told Rebekah that she was having twins, it must have come as a huge surprise. These were the first-ever recorded twins in the Bible. This blessing broke the mold. Twins were uncommon and extraordinary. What God was essentially saying to Rebekah, and to you today, is "I'm going to do something through you, that's never been done before—something extraordinary." The reason there's such a struggle is because God wants to bless you like never before, touch you like never before, and use you like never before. You have an extraordinary purpose in your life.

Be encouraged today. Know that God has chosen you and what you're going through could be just a sign of your divine destiny. There's nothing common about your role in God's plan. Within you lies a gift, a ministry, or a dream that can change your world.

Lord, We Need to Talk

Rebekah never pretended to have all the answers. I guess that's what I like about her. She was authentic and humble. When she didn't know what do to, she came before God and admitted that she needed help. Rebekah inquired of the Lord.

When faced with uncertainty and questions about her life, she looked to God for the answers. It pains the heart of God when we look everywhere else but him for the solution to our problems. Notice how open God was with her. He spoke to her like a friend. As I bring this chapter to a close, I invite you to examine your relationship with God.

I'm not questioning whether or not you pray. To be fair, I'll assume that you have a prayer life of some degree. Here's my real question; how open are you with Him? Sometimes we demand answers and openness from God, without first being open ourselves. When Rebekah came before the Lord, she put all her laundry on the table. She didn't just spend an hour recycling a tired prayer. She bore her soul and lifted the veil off her frustrations—basically saying, "God, you blessed me, but why do I feel so terrible? Why can't I just be happy?"

When you begin pray honestly, you shed the rehearsed idioms and say what's really on your mind. Isn't it time you got that issue off your chest? Isn't it time that you tell the Lord how you really feel. Trust me. He already knows. He's just waiting for you to let go and get real with him.

I wish I could tell you that Rebekah's life was easy after her children were born. I wish I could say that she never had another heartache, another challenge, or another disappointment. The reality is that she learned how to survive and maintain her joy in spite of her circumstances.

There would be more disappointments and challenges down the road. However, at anytime she could pull over and say, "Lord, can we talk?" It's that connection with God that will carry you through life's peaks and valleys.

Chapter 20

Maid for More

Big things come in small packages—they really do. People love to hear stories of how the little guys beat the big guys. We're fascinated by stories like David and Goliath. We crave the adventure of people little in stature or status accomplishing big things. Perhaps this appeal comes from the fact that we can identify with them, and when we see their character, we catch a frame of who we are. Some of the greatest heroes and heroines of our time are common people who dared to dream and challenge their limitations.

Many unlikely people have turned the tide of history and changed the world as we know it. I would like to share some insights about a young insignificant girl who made a significant impact.

In 2 Kings 5:2-3, we find the following story: *"Now groups of Aramean raiders had invaded the land of Israel, and among their captives was a young girl who had been given to Naaman's wife as a maid. One day the girl said to her mistress, "I wish my master would go to see the prophet in Samaria. He would heal him of his leprosy."*

Nestled in the book of Second Kings is a brief glance at a life rarely discussed, the life of the little maid. Her story can be easily overlooked because her life and history are captured in only a couple of sentences. Imagine that! Her whole existence is summed up in two sentences. That's something to ponder. It's easy to know what kind of person Ruth was because a whole book is dedicated to her, with four chapters of historical settings, monologues, dialogues and scenes. Would Ruth be as well remembered if her story had been told in two sentences? Or imagine telling your entire life story in two short sentences? What would you say?

The girl in the story wasn't some superstar. She was little. She was a servant. She was inexperienced. She was nameless. She's only known in the Bible as the little maid, or the servant girl. You will find out how this little woman sparked a big event for someone other than herself. You'll see a person who changed her life and the lives of others in a positive way.

We can only imagine what the little girl's life was like before being captured. We can logically assume a few things: She had a home, more than likely a family as well. Like any young girl in those days, her life was simple and dependent upon her parents. She probably played with her friends and did a few household chores. Nothing too extraordinary.

Then, on a day that began like any other, her life was radically changed. Invaders came into her village and home, raiding the land. They took what could be taken, including people. In a matter of moments, her entire life was turned upside down. She was taken out of the comfort and love and safety of her home and family, removed from all that had made her feel secure. There is no pretty wrapping paper to cover up what really happened. She became a slave—living with strangers and serving their needs. What a scary feeling—especially for an adolescent. She had to learn the language, the culture and the customs. That's a lot for anyone to experience. Her situation forced her to survive in an uncomfortable and frightening place.

Although security uncertain and life is full of changes, you can still become the wonderful woman God created you to be. In reality, the events that took place in the maid's life, though they were hostile, actually prepared her for a noble purpose.

Isn't that the way life unfolds? Trouble strikes and we feel like our lives are ruined, then in the midst of the situation, we find a truer sense of purpose.

Real purpose is often hidden under the rocks of real pressure. Sometimes we fail to see our true destiny because we run from trouble and dodge life-changing circumstances. I don't suggest you look for trouble, but when it comes, search for a way to grow and learn.

The fact that this girl's life changed so dramatically was actually minor compared to the significant role God had for her. The title of this chapter is meaningful. I did a play on the word "made" and changed it to "maid" to emphasize the girl's literal role and purpose. She became a maid and was made for more than she could ever imagine.

Wanting More Out of Life

Your life is not just the result of coincidental events. Life is not just about where you've been and where you are now. Life is about where you're going.

People too often approach life with a nonchalant perspective. Eventually life's activities become so structured that each step is like a rehearsed dance. For millions, life is only about getting up, going to work, paying the bills, eating, watching their favorite TV show and going back to bed. Then the same routine is followed the next day.

Daily living can become such a scripted routine that people don't even consider the idea that there could be more. Is there more to life than just clocking in and out of work? Could there be more to life than going from weekend to weekend, paycheck to paycheck, vacation to vacation?

Is there more?

I'm discovering that people, even Christian women, live methodical lives with no sense of something more. They settle for less and feel excluded from opportunities to minister. God has more for you than you can imagine. His purposes are endless and His plans are amazing. He made you to be a great woman, a woman who isn't confined to tradition or subject to average existence.

It's time to unwrap, and even unpack the gifts and potential that God has placed in you. God wants to give you more. He really does. He wants you to experience the treasures that He has for you. Imagine that God has a "more box," a chest in heaven filled with priceless things that will add more to your life. Maybe He wants to give you more, but He can't because you haven't searched enough, prayed enough, or even cared enough.

Life is as meaningful and colorful as you make it. I often hear people say that they're waiting for God to show them their purpose. I also hear people say that they're praying for God to give them a ministry or to open some mysterious door. We often view purpose as some mystifying endowment. In reality, purpose is standing right in front of us. You were made for more. Your mind, body and spirit were designed for more than daily routines.

Here's an interesting way of viewing the power of more. Since technology is such a part of our world, I'll use a fitting analogy. Say you own a computer (I presume you do), and all you ever use is its clock. That would be quite an expensive clock. If that's all you use, the computer has no problem running that function—it's probably the simplest element on your desktop. There's absolutely nothing wrong with using the clock; however, is your computer being used to its fullest potential? Is there more you could be doing with it? Your computer can operate programs, send e-mails, create documents, design art, and so much more. There is so much more you can do with your computer when you know its potential and understand how to use it. If life was a computer, and all you did was use the clock, you would be missing out on great things.

What part of your life has become your "clock"—a rut where you are stuck, a focus that is keeping you from reaching your potential? Your "clock" may be a job, a hobby or any activity or relationship that absorbs all your energy. Life is a robust system with endless opportunities. Don't waste your time staring at the "clock." You have potential. You have more than you realize. Being a woman is not a liability, but an asset to your destiny.

*Miss*fortunes

The servant girl didn't choose her circumstances. She was thrown into a situation that was literally beyond her control. She had no choice. All she could do was accept her new lifestyle. Her security had been taken, her childhood had been robbed and her parents were gone. This girl's whole world was turned upside down.

I would describe her case as a severe misfortune, or more fittingly—a *missfortune*. There was nothing appealing about becoming a servant, even if it was to a famous family. Work is work. A servant is a servant. If she didn't know how to cook, she had to learn. If she didn't know how to sew, she had to learn. If she had no clue how to clean, wash, care, nurse or serve an affluent family, she had to learn. Despite her resentment or sadness, the only way this girl could be happy was to make the best of a sour situation.

I've discovered that some of the greatest women were those who were forced to overcome adversity. Many successful businesswomen have experienced raw deals and even bankruptcy. Many thriving entrepreneurs fail repeatedly and suffered hardship before finally achieving success.

Misfortune happens. And you'll find that it happens more then a couple of times during your life. The question to ask today is not, "Will I experience misfortune?" but rather, "What will I do when I experience misfortune?" It's what you do with difficult circumstances that determine your success in life.

Someone once coined the phrase, "When life gives you lemons, make lemonade." The saying is witty, yet entirely true. Sometimes life is going to hand you a lemon, maybe even a whole basket of them! The more lemons you receive, the more lemonade you have to make. Turning sour lemons into sweet lemonade is taking something negative and making it positive.

To capture more of life, you must determine to make lemonade out of lemons. You have to decide that no matter what, you're moving on. It's easy to throw in the towel. It's easy to wallow in sadness and give up. But the possibilities are endless for the woman who adopts a positive attitude.

Following Her Steps

The bible is filled with women who experienced misfortunes, yet they learned to maximize them. The bible's most inspirational women are those who overcome problem after problem and learned how to make lemonade out of life's lemons. Let's review the women with misfortunes that you've read about in this book:

- Leah was unloved
- Gomer was unfaithful
- Jochebed's situation was unfair

- Sarah was unsure of herself

- Ruth was uncertain

- Rebekah was unhappy at times

Yet all these women were blessed because of God's perfect strength in their hearts. Unfair things will surface anywhere greatness is brewed. The key is to make the most of your troubles and to take advantage of any opportunity that God offers. The servant girl is a prime example of making positive use of a great misfortune.

I hope the closing chapters of this book will polish your outlook on life. I sometimes think that the myriad of "how-to" books on the bookshelves make it tougher, rather than easier, to understand what life is all about. We'll look at some final steps you can take to live the life God designed for you and receive His prefect strength.

Chapter 21

Unveiling your Hidden Power

Someone is watching you, and your character is center stage. Abraham Lincoln once said, "Character is like a tree and reputation like a shadow. The shadow is what we think of it; the tree is the real thing." Nothing will remain in the minds of others more than your character, which happens to be your hidden power. Character is what turns good women into great women. Character defines you. It gives you a priceless value and unlocks God's strength in your life. Skills and determination nurture your potential, but it is your character that nurtures your legacy.

The story of the little maid unveils her power of her character. Although we don't see the growth of her character, we see the fruit of it. When she saw her master's need, she could have stayed silent. She was only a servant; nothing on her job description said anything about speaking faith to her masters. The girl didn't have to speak one word, yet she chose to do the right thing. She chose to help someone who probably didn't deserve it.

Character is about walking the talk, or simply practicing what you preach. I have found that it is always easier to teach principles from behind a pulpit than it is to live them. Walking out your words is not easy, but when you have character, you understand it's vital.

If you achieve great things without the core of character, you will find success to be short-lived. Without a moral foundation, efforts to succeed will be overshadowed by the temptation to compromise. A solid character will manifest unwavering convictions and beliefs. It will balance your appetite for success, giving you a compass for every decision you make.

In most cases, character isn't really noticed until it's tested. Character is exhibited through crisis and conflict. In other words, true character, or its lack, always reveals itself when the heat is on.

When faced with a risky decision or tough situation, your character will manifest. As long as everything is "business as usual" and things are rolling smoothly, your character is quiet. But as soon as your life is challenged, your true character will shine.

Developed in the Dark

Character is an invisible virtue with visible value. It is not tangible or touchable, but it always materializes. It's something that exhibits itself—usually when you're not aware of it. Your character will never warn you and say, "Hey, be careful, someone's watching." It simply shows. Like a photograph, character is displayed in the open, but it's developed in the dark, the unseen areas of your life.

Character is a discipline, not a gift—something you work on daily. God doesn't hand out gifts of character. Rather it comes through a process of learning, growing and yielding to God. Your gifts and talents will create opportunities. However, your character will influence what you do when those opportunities arise.

People will always remember you more for who you are than for what you have done.

Take a moment to think of someone you greatly admire. It could be your father, mother, mentor, friend or anyone else. Identify what you admire most about this person. Perhaps it's tough to pinpoint just one thing, but try to narrow it down. Now, let me ask you this question: Is the quality you admire most, one that reflects accomplishments (i.e. occupation, hobbies, financial successes, etc.), or character traits (i.e. honest, caring, brave, etc.)? I'm willing to bet that that you most admire the kind of person this is—his or her character traits.

Character has nearly nothing to do with what you do and everything to do with who you are. Contrary to popular opinion, who you are, not what you do, is what people will admire most about you.

Proverbs 11:3 says, *"The integrity of the upright shall guide them: but the perverseness of transgressors shall destroy them"*. Integrity is the desire to do what's moral or ethical even when it's tough. The issue of integrity is far from popular. In the corporate world, academia and even religious arenas, integrity should be our foundation.

Here are a few suggestions to develop your character:

1. Learn from Christ

In Jesus Christ we discover all that is holy, moral, just, righteous and pure. By learning and applying the traits of Christ, our character will grow in beautiful ways. Read the gospels of Matthew, Mark, Luke and John. Study how Jesus behaved. Observe how He handled hot topics and sticky situations. Pay close attention to how He dealt with people's attitudes and skirmishes. Study His teachings. Read until you get a view of His heart. Consider how He responded to criticism, judgment, dishonesty, deception and cruelty. In other words, get to know Christ, and you'll know character. By drawing from His example, you will understand what good character is.

2. Lean not to your understanding

In Proverbs 3:5-6 we read, *"Trust in the LORD with all your heart, and lean not on your own understanding; in all your ways acknowledge Him, and He shall direct your paths"*. The fast lane to poor character is refusing counsel. Those who feel they know everything are sure to be trapped by something. Human wisdom can be frail and at times misguided, but God's wisdom is powerful and life changing.

Should you ever have doubts, don't be afraid to ask for help. Cultivating your character involves a process of obtaining godly wisdom for daily decisions. Some of the greatest women of character are those who weren't too proud to stop and ask for directions.

Maybe it's a male thing, but I don't like pulling over and asking for directions. Admitting that I don't know where I'm headed is humbling. I'd rather miss a couple of turns than to ask some gas station clerk. I know—it's silly. However, when it comes to decisions and choices that affect my family, my reputation or my ministry, I must pull over and ask for counsel. Proverbs 20:5 states, *"Counsel in the heart of man is like deep water, but a man of understanding will draw it out"*.

3. Look in the mirror

Evaluation is the key to escalation. Don't be afraid to look at your life in the mirror. The woman who refuses to examine herself is not willing to face reality. We often fear the mirror of introspection because we're afraid of what we might see. We're afraid to confront our immaturities, inconsistencies, and even insecurities. Don't be afraid to face your unhealthy habits or traits. It's easy to fly on autopilot and ignore the real issues. However, it is crucial for you to understand that the strength of your in-look determines the strength of your outlook.

I'm reminded of the time that David cried these words, *"Search me, O God, and know my heart: try me, and know my thoughts: And see if there be any wicked way in me, and lead me in the way everlasting"* (Psalm 139:23, 24 KJV). Self-examination isn't for those who presume failure—it's for those who pursue success. If you aren't already practicing this, begin today. Through prayer, ask God to show you areas in your life that need improvement. Then ask Him to help you fortify your character. Gradually you'll begin to notice a change.

The Key to God's Favor

The little maid was willing to do the right thing, even if it wasn't her place to speak. This young girl had to make a choice. "Am I going to say something, or am I going to keep silent?"

Character is doing the right thing, no matter what cost or risk is involved. When you were a child, did telling a lie sometimes seem like the easiest path to take? If you broke your mother's favorite vase, denying guilt might have felt better at the moment, but eventually your lie probably caught up to you. Then, instead of being punished just for breaking the vase, you were punished for lying too. Practicing integrity may have its initial sting, but doing the right thing always pays off in the long run.

Allow me to deviate from my "women only" examples throughout this book, and shine the spotlight on Joseph's encounter with Potiphar's wife. This is a powerful illustration of being willing to suffer for doing the right thing. As a young man, Joseph was seduced by his master's wife, but he stood firm in his convictions. When Potiphar's wife sashayed around Joseph with her batting eyelashes and scented fragrance, his character was being tested.

Day after day, she tried to seduce Joseph and lure him into her bedroom. Yet every time she would pressure him, he refused. A man with no integrity or moral character might have consented, but because Joseph was a godly, moral man, he continued to resist her flirtations. The result: he was falsely accused, demoted and imprisoned (Ref. Genesis 39:10-20).

How can this be? How could a man who did the right thing be treated this way?

Joseph's immediate reward for righteousness was a prison sentence. In his case, displaying character was costly. Doing the honorable thing cost Joseph his freedom.

We'll all encounter a "Potiphar's wife" sooner or later. Potiphar's wife represents temptation, seducing spirits, sin and immorality. Your Potiphar's wife may not be a sensual matter, but perhaps a business or ministry choice. She could present herself in various ways. Her batting eyelashes might be the lust for financial gain. Her pungent fragrance might be the enticement of personal pleasure. Whatever form Potiphar's wife takes in your life, resist. At all costs, resist. If it means demotion and denial, resist. If it means a prison of suffering is to be your new home, continue to resist. As you'll see in the following verses, the long-term reward will be worth the cost:

"But the LORD was with Joseph there, too, and he granted Joseph favor with the chief jailer. Before long, the jailer put Joseph in charge of all the other prisoners and over everything that happened in the prison. The chief jailer had no more worries after that, because Joseph took care of everything. The LORD was with him, making everything run smoothly and successfully" (Genesis 39:21-23, NLT).

Character always prevails. Potiphar's wife probably presumed that Joseph was finished; however, it was quite the opposite. God is more concerned about holiness and character than gifts, talents, anointing or position. He gives favor to the upright. The key to God's favor is resisting sin and standing for what's right. Sure, Joseph suffered a little bit, but his suffering wasn't in vain. While hidden in the prison, the Lord was with him.

I love the way the verse following Joseph's imprisonment begins with, *"But the LORD was with Joseph there, too."* Satan, the jokes on you! God abides near those who uphold morality and holiness. While sleeping behind prison walls, God was with him. I'd rather be imprisoned with God than free to walk without Him. Character costs—but its benefits always pay off. You might not see the results of the decisions and choices you're making right now for ten to fifteen years, or maybe not even this side of heaven. But know that choosing God's way is right and pleases your Father and opens the door to His blessings.

Joseph was anointed, gifted and chosen, but without the character to make the right decisions, his destiny would have been cancelled. To ensure God's favor upon your life, grow in character and God will bless your path.

Chapter 22

Living Beyond Yourself

There is a practical element to the servant girl's story that we can't miss. Let's not forget her fundamental role. She was a servant, a maid in her master's house. She was in a position where she had to live beyond herself. Even though God used her to communicate a great message of hope, she still had to dust off the tables, wash the floors and tend to her master's needs. Her life wasn't easy. I'm not even sure she got promoted after her role in Naaman's miracle. I assume she kept on serving.

Serving is a beautiful privilege in the body of Christ. So much can be said of its power and purpose. Christ himself modeled a servant's role like no other. At the core of every servant of Christ is humility. In order to be a servant, one must be humble in spirit. Being humble is not being weak, broke, shy or timid, as people often think. In fact, humility has nothing to do with how much money you have—you can be bankrupt and still have a proud spirit.

Humble Endings

I called this section "humble endings" because typically we talk about the figure of speech, "humble beginnings". What difference does it make to start off humble, only to become proud? The reality is, we need to stay humble, no matter what level of success we achieve.

Humility doesn't equal weakness; however, it does equal meekness. Meekness is not weakness; rather it is controlled strength. Being humble doesn't mean being insecure—some of the most humble people I know are very confident. Great blessings follow those who are humble. To truly understand humility, you must remember what pride is. Pride is contrary to humility. The bible speaks loud and clear about pride.

- Pride is sin (Proverbs 21:4)
- Hateful to God (Proverbs 6:16-17)
- Hardens the mind (Daniel 5:20)
- Keeps from seeking God (Psalm 10:4)
- Leads to destruction (Proverbs 16:18)
- Worthy of punishment (Malachi 4:1)

This is a small list compared to everything the Bible says. One scripture that helps my perspective is Proverbs 18:12, *"Before destruction the heart of a man is haughty, and before honor is humility"*. This tells us exactly what both pride and humility produces. If your heart is proud (arrogant, high minded, above obedience or self-righteous), expect failure. It's coming. God promises that pride will produce destruction. However, if your heart is humble (lowly, submissive, teachable, caring or meek), you may expect honor. The plumpest fruit of humility is honor, from both God and people.

Being a servant is more than just getting the job done. It's more than just fulfilling a task or assignment. Being a true servant requires having a humble heart. God is more interested in a woman's heart than her performance. God looks into the intent of our hearts. Additionally, God will bless a humble heart. In Matthew 5:3 Jesus says, *"Blessed are the poor in spirit: for theirs is the kingdom of heaven"*. The term poor in spirit refers to unvarnished humility. Those who are humble shall inherent the kingdom of heaven. This is a promise of God! If you walk humbly and live lowly in spirit, Christ will give you kingdom power and authority.

Service with a Smile

To be a true servant, you must find satisfaction in serving. A study of the bible's most celebrated characters, including women, reveals that many of them were workers at heart. Remember the story of Rebekah, and how she served water to Eliezer. That was no easy task. Yet, in doing so, it positioned her for greatness. In fact, her attitude of serving someone else before herself was her true test of character.

Eliezer said, *"Behold, here I stand by the well of water, and the daughters of the men of the city are coming out to draw water. Now let it be that the young woman to whom I say, 'Please let down your pitcher that I may drink,' and she says, 'Drink, and I will also give your camels a drink'—let her be the one You have appointed for Your servant Isaac. And by this I will know that You have shown kindness to my master"*(Genesis 24:13-14).

When Eliezer came at the well, he prayed for a sign that would reveal Isaac's bride. Service was the sign. Imagine what possibilities await those who serve?

If Jesus' ministry included washing people's feet, as well as raising people from the dead, why should our lives be any different? Jesus Christ didn't see serving as a burdensome chore—He saw it as a privilege. He didn't serve with an attitude or a secret agenda. Christ served with meekness, grace, mercy and love. To Him, it was an absolute honor to kneel on the rough floor and bathe the feet of his own students.

How many Ivy League professors would stoop down and clean their students' feet? How many CEO's would roll up their French cuffs, kneel and serve their people? Jesus, being both the ultimate teacher and CEO of the galaxy, girded Himself with a towel and submerged his hands in a basin. He is the Savior and the Servant. What a great model we have in Christ—who lived beyond Himself.

A servant must understand the concept of giving and personal sacrifice. Servanthood is all putting others first. A great example of this is found in the union of marriage. Marriage is about more than holding hands and cuddling. Marriage is serving. A husband serves his wife, and a wife serves her husband. As husband to my wife Cherie, I must put her needs before mine. All that I have, I freely give to her. And when I give to her, whether time or strength, I'm not reluctant or bitter.

The glue is love. As a servant, you must love those you're serving. This is why God loves a cheerful giver. He adores someone who not only gives, but gives with joy and happiness. Serving must be a joy to you. Sure, it may be uncomfortable and challenging at times. But as long as your heart is generous, your service will be rewarding. Jesus Christ demonstrates charity like no other. We see a direct association with the Lord's love and His willingness to give. John 3:16 tells us, *"For God so loved the world that He gave His only begotten Son, that whoever believes in Him should not perish but have everlasting life"*.

Keep the Right Attitude

A huge part of serving depends on your attitude. President Thomas Jefferson commented, *"Nothing can stop the man with the right mental attitude from achieving his goal; nothing on earth can help the man with the wrong mental attitude."*

A prime example of positive attitude versus negative attitude is found in the Old Testament story of the twelve Israelite spies entering the land of Canaan. Moses sent a team of moles into their promised land to scope out territory and to explore every detail. The Israelite people were preparing to possess the land that God had promised them. They were excited and ready for something great. The plan was for the moles to identify the strongholds so that a winning strategy could be assembled to possess the land (Ref. Numbers 13).

The spies returned with two very different attitudes. Ten of them reported negative and unfavorable news. And only two of them, Joshua and Caleb, testified that the land was attainable. Without getting into the reasons why the other ten were so negative, the most important element is the way their negativity spread. At the moment they demonstrated a bad attitude, the entire nation was affected.

Within hours, everyone was disappointed and doubtful. Although Joshua and Caleb expressed a very enthusiastic attitude, the people quickly leaned toward the negative. Their response demonstrates how a poor attitude compounds more efficiently than a healthy one. The people of Israel mourned over a battle that hadn't even been fought yet. They wept bitterly because of the influence of some negative spies.

Keeping a positive attitude is not based on how you feel. We often lean on our feelings and allow them to direct our decisions. But, feelings are fickle. If you let your feelings dictate your attitude, your personal potential will be limited. Base your attitude on God's goodness and purpose.

The possibility of serving with success hinges on attitude. Having the right attitude determines how well you handle success and how long your success will last. If success is the open door, attitude is the hinge. Success hinges on attitude. With that in mind, attitude must be seen as a discipline, not something you're born with.

Attitude is a discipline because it must be worked on daily. The more you work on it, the better it will become.

Life is filled with uncertainties and changes. In order for you to experience and enjoy the life God has given you, you have to have the right attitude. If not, you'll stay stuck in the same place, never seeing your dreams come to life. Choose to see the light, even when things are dark. Successful people are not those who avoid adversity and dodge the need for adjustment, but individuals who face challenges and see adversity as an opportunity for growth.

No matter how much strength God has for you as His daughter, your attitude and spirit determine how much you will receive.

The servant girl, as disheartening as her situation was, kept the right attitude. And her positive attitude caused her to rise to the occasion. Her attitude was not something she was born with, neither is it something you and I were born with. A good attitude, like any other characteristic, must be cultivated. Most importantly, your attitude will help you see and live beyond yourself. It will help you focus on other people's needs, rather than your own. It will cause to you invest in someone else, before expecting someone to invest in you.

The right attitude could be the very thing God needs to bless your life and those you love. It's the link to making the most of God's prefect strength.

Epilogue

Congratulations for completing this book. From the moment I began to write the first chapter, I knew something special was happening. The women you met in these pages, both familiar and unfamiliar, are like threads woven into God's tapestry of strength. Although they lived in ancient times, their lives still speak today. Perhaps that is what life is all about—not what is thought of you today, but what is remembered of you tomorrow.

Nevertheless, I commend you for reading all the way through. My secret hope is that you not only learned more about these seven women, but more about you. I think there is something in each woman you can relate to. Why? Because you and other women are not so different than you think.

I encourage you to flip back through the pages and re-read those areas of application that were presented in each chapter. Maybe you missed something. Maybe you skimmed past an area where the Holy Ghost wanted more time to work. Or perhaps you need to reread a certain chapter that touched on some sensitive issues in your life. Either way, don't let this resource become a dust collector. You can start a discussion group, give a bible study, or even lend this resource to a friend.

This book was birthed out of an ever-growing desire to minister to God's people. I pray that it made an impact on your life.

About the Author

Jacob M. Rodriguez is the founder and pastor of CityLight Church in Mountain View, California. His dynamic sermons and books reach a global audience and touch thousands of people. He has written eight books, including *The Lord's Lady*, *Shift* and *Lying Lions*. Jacob and his wife, Cherie, have two wonderful children, Makai and Chloe.

To learn more about Jacob's ministry, visit his website at www.jacobrodriguez.org. Or to learn more about CityLight Church, visit www.citylightonline.org.

24063961R00175

Made in the USA
Middletown, DE
13 September 2015